JOYRIDERS & TEA IN A CHINA CUP

'*Tea in a China Cup,* Christina Reid's prize-winning [...]
Protestant family between 1939 and 1972 is no more [...]
a fiercely proud working-class keeping up appearance [...] their men
off to war, laying out the dead of the last generation w....c aspiring to better things
for the next, and the obsessive domestic trappings that limit the women's horizons.
Three-quarters of the way through violence erupts off-stage. . . by which time it is
perfectly set in the context of the gritty life-style of a part of the UK to many of us,
shamefully, more foreign than Middle America.'

Martin Hoyle, *Financial Times*

'. . . lovely play, moving and passionate without ever needing to raise its voice . . . what
emerges from this affectionate domestic chronicle is Ms Reid's alarm at women's
acquiescent role, a theme that boldly holds together a big span of subjects from the
most public to the most personal.'

Anthony Masters, *The Times*

'the fabric and cement of this matriarchal Belfast community is beautifully sketched
in with its anti-Catholic prejudices, its driving demand for respectability (symbolised
by the household's pride and joy, the china tea cup set), its superstitious rituals, and
most of all, its resilient, sometimes irreverent humour . . .'

Carole Woddis, *City Limits*

'That Ireland also remains the country where the wrong people run out between the
guns and get themselves shot is the matter of Christina Reid's very sparky new play
Joyriders. . . . Four kids from the Divis flats in west Belfast, working on a year's
youth opportunity project for probationers on suspended sentence, sneer and snigger
and blub their way through O'Casey's *Shadow of a Gunman*, whose tragic events are
repeated with unpredicted and absolute plausibility at the end of Ms Reid's play.
There is a little optimism and even some justice, and the piece is often very funny
indeed . . .'

Michael Ratcliffe, *The Observer*

'Belfast playwright Christina Reid writes passionately and emotionally about the
daily degradations of Belfast youth — her direct, lyrical dialogue capturing the
idiom of a people whose Troubles far from making them self-indulgent force on them
a crystal clear realism.'

Suzie Mackenzie, *Time Out*

'. . . a new hard-headed drama is coming out of Ireland.'

Irving Wardle, *The Times*

The front cover photos show (top, left to right) Clare Cathcart, Fabian Cartwright,
Veronica Duffy, Gerard O'Hare and Michelle Fairley in the Paines Plough production
of *Joyriders* (photo: Sarah Ainslie) and (below) Stella McCusker and Paula Hamilton
in the Lyric Theatre Belfast production of *Tea in a China Cup* (photo: Chris Hill).

in the same series

A COLDER CLIMATE
by Karim Alrawi
BURIED INSIDE EXTRA
by Thomas Babe
THE LUCKY CHANCE
by Aphra Behn
DEREK & CHORUSES FROM AFTER THE
    ASSASSINATIONS
THE WAR PLAYS:
    PARTS ONE & TWO
    PART THREE
HUMAN CANNON
by Edward Bond
THE GENIUS
by Howard Brenton
THIRTEENTH NIGHT & A SHORT SHARP
    SHOCK!
by Howard Brenton (*A Short Sharp Shock!*
    written with Tony Howard)
SLEEPING POLICEMEN
by Howard Brenton and Tunde Ikoli
MOLIÈRE
by Mikhail Bulgakov (in a version by Dusty
    Hughes)
MONEY
by Edward Bulwer-Lytton
RETURN TO THE FORBIDDEN PLANET
by Bob Carlton
ROAD
by Jim Cartwright
THE SEAGULL
by Anton Chekhov (in a version by Thomas
    Kilroy)
SHONA, LUNCH GIRLS, THE SHELTER
by Tony Craze, Ron Hart, Johnnie Quarrell
NEAPTIDE
RIPEN OUR DARKNESS & THE DEVIL'S
    GATEWAY
by Sarah Daniels
THE BODY
by Nick Darke
WRECKERS
ENTERTAINING STRANGERS
by David Edgar
TORCH SONG TRILOGY
by Harvey Fierstein
OUR FRIENDS IN THE NORTH
by Peter Flannery
RUMBLINGS
by Peter Gibbs
THE GOVERNMENT INSPECTOR
by Nikolai Gogol (in a version by
    Adrian Mitchell)
MAKING NOISE QUIETLY
OTHER WORLDS
THE OVERGROWN PATH
TODAY
by Robert Holman
THE RED DEVILS TRILOGY
by Debbie Horsfield
RAT IN THE SKULL
by Ron Hutchinson
PEER GYNT
by Henrik Ibsen (translated by David Rudkin)
CRIES FROM THE MAMMAL HOUSE
INSIGNIFICANCE
TUESDAY'S CHILD & TIME TROUBLE
(*Tuesday's Child* written with Kate Lock)
by Terry Johnson
BASTARD ANGEL
BETTER TIMES
SUS
by Barrie Keeffe
THE 1984 VERITY BARGATE AWARD
    SHORT PLAYS
(*Up for None* by Mick Mahoney &
Coming Apart by Melissa Murray
Edited by Barrie Keeffe)
NOT QUITE JERUSALEM
by Paul Kember
THE NORMAL HEART
by Larry Kramer

BORDERLINE
by Hanif Kureishi
TOUCHED
TIBETAN INROADS
THE RAGGED TROUSERED
    PHILANTHROPISTS
MOVING PICTURES
(*Moving Pictures, Seachange, Stars, Strive*)
by Stephen Lowe
PROGRESS & HARD FEELINGS
by Doug Lucie
LAVENDER BLUE & NOLI ME TANGERE
by John Mackendrick
EDMOND
by David Mamet
THICK AS THIEVES
WELCOME HOME, RASPBERRY, THE
    LUCKY ONES
by Tony Marchant
A NEW WAY TO PAY OLD DEBTS
by Philip Massinger
PLAY MAS, INDEPENDENCE &
    MEETINGS
by Mustapha Matura
LUNATIC AND LOVER
by Michael Meyer
MADE IN BANGKOK
by Anthony Minghella
OPERATION BAD APPLE
AN HONOURABLE TRADE
by G.F. Newman
BEAUTY AND THE BEAST
REAL ESTATE
SALONIKA
by Louise Page
ONE FOR THE ROAD
by Harold Pinter
STRAWBERRY FIELDS
SHOUT ACROSS THE RIVER
AMERICAN DAYS
THE SUMMER PARTY
FAVOURITE NIGHTS & CAUGHT ON A
    TRAIN
RUNNERS & SOFT TARGETS
by Stephen Poliakoff
THE TIME OF YOUR LIFE
by William Saroyan
SPELL NUMBER SEVEN
by Ntozake Shange
MY DINNER WITH ANDRÉ & MARIE AND
    BRUCE
by Wallace Shaw (*My Dinner with André*
    written with André Gregory)
HOW THE VOTE WAS WON and other
    Suffragette plays
an anthology edited by Dale Spender and
    Carole Hayman
LIVE THEATRE: Four Plays for Young
    People
by C.P. Taylor
BAZAAR AND RUMMAGE, GROPING
    FOR WORDS & WOMBERANG
THE GREAT CELESTIAL COW
by Sue Townsend
CLAY
by Peter Whelan
THE NINE NIGHT & RITUAL BY WATER
by Edgar White
RENTS
LENT
by David Wilcox
SUGAR AND SPICE & TRIAL RUN
W.C.P.C.
by Nigel Williams
THE GRASS WIDOW
by Snoo Wilson
HAS 'WASHINGTON' LEGS? & DINGO
by Charles Wood
THE DESERT AIR
CUSTOM OF THE COUNTRY
by Nicholas Wright

JOYRIDERS

&

TEA IN A CHINA CUP

Two Belfast Plays by

CHRISTINA REID

A Methuen Paperback

For Christina my mother, and my daughters Heidi, Tara and Siubhan.

*And my thanks to The Lyric Theatre Belfast; Paines Plough The Writers
Company; Divis Community Centre; Eileen O'Casey; Leaflyn Jones. And my special
love and thanks to Phil Kelvin for her faith and her friendship.*

A Methuen Theatrescript

First published in Great Britain and Northern Ireland as a Methuen Paperback original
in 1987 by Methuen London Ltd, 11 New Fetter Lane, London EC4P 4EE and in the
United States of America by Methuen Inc, 29 West 35th Street, New York NY 10001

Acknowledgement
The extract from *Shadow of a Gunman* by Sean O'Casey was taken from *Sean
O'Casey — Collected Plays Vol. I* and is reproduced by kind permission of
Macmillan Ltd., London and Basingstoke.

Set in 10pt IBM Press Roman by Tek-Art 🅰 Croydon, Surrey
Printed in Great Britain

British Library Cataloguing in Publication Data
Reid, Christina
    Joyriders; &, Tea in a china cup.
    1. Title
    822' .914 PR6068.E42/
    ISBN 0-413-14780-0

TEA IN A CHINA CUP

Tea in a China Cup was first produced by the Lyric Players Theatre Belfast on 9 November 1983, with the following cast:

SARAH	Stella McCusker
BETH, *Sarah's daughter*	Paula Hamilton
THERESA, *Beth's friend*	Frances Quinn
THE GRANDMOTHER	Trudy Kelly
THE GRANDFATHER	Louis Rolston
GREAT AUNT MAISIE	Sheila McGibbon
SAMUEL, *Sarah's brother* SAMMY, *Sarah's son* A YOUTH	Adrian Gordon
COUNCIL CLERK FORTUNE TELLER MRS JAMISON	Margaret D'Arcy
ARMY OFFICER, *Second World War* MODERN BRITISH SOLDIER VALUER	John Hewitt

NOTE. In this production only, the valuer in the final scene was male and became female in subsequent productions following re-writes.

Director Leon Rubin   *Set Construction* Jim Carson
Set Designer Ken Harrison   *Stage Manager* Rose Morris
Lighting Designer Trevor Dawson   *Deputy Stage Manager* Karen Kerr
Costume Designer Ivor C. Morrow   *Assistant Stage Manager* Maggie Burge
Wardrobe   Jacqueline Berryman   *Acting Assistant Stage Manager*
         Ivor C. Morrow   Adrian Gordon

The action of the play is set in Belfast and spans more than three decades (from 1939–1972), in the life of a Protestant family in Belfast.

A velvet sofa symbolises Beth's elegant house.

A china cabinet plus three large framed photographs of: the grandfather in First World War uniform; his son Samuel in Second World War uniform; his grandson Sammy in modern army uniform, symbolise the little house that is occupied first of all by the grandparents and subsequently by Sarah.

Changes of lighting indicate changes of time and place.

The play is in two acts.

ACT ONE

The stage is in darkness. Offstage, in the distance is heard the sound of an Orange band playing 'Up Come the Man'. As the music increases in volume, stage left lightens to show a velvet sofa by a window. This is BETH's *house in 1972.* BETH's *mother,* SARAH, *a woman in her mid-fifties, walks slowly out of the darkened stage area and lies down on the velvet sofa. She is wearing a dressing gown, and is obviously very ill. She listens to and watches the Orange band as it passes by with great enjoyment. Offstage a crowd is heard singing and cheering 'Up come the man with the shovel in his hand, and he says boys go no farther, for we'll get a great big rope and we'll hang the bloody Pope, on the twelfth of July in the morning'. The music and singing increase as the band marches past.* SARAH *sinks back on the sofa and closes her eyes. She smiles and sings softly to herself 'Up comes the man with the shovel in his hand . . . and he says . . . boys go no farther . . .' The lights darken around* SARAH *and lighten on stage right where* BETH *is standing at a desk facing a female* COUNCIL CLERK.

BETH (*nervously*): I want to buy a grave . . .

CLERK (*briskly*): It'll have to be in the new cemetery, the old one's full, you know.

BETH: Yes, I know.

CLERK: A single or a double?

BETH: What?

CLERK: Plot . . . a single or a double?

BETH: A single . . . please . . .

CLERK: When's the burial?

BETH: The burial?

CLERK: The time and date of the funeral?

BETH: I don't know . . .

CLERK: Today's Friday, this office closes at the weekend you know. If the interment is to be on Monday you'll have to arrange for the grave to be opened today.

BETH: Oh, I don't want it opened . . . not now . . . not yet . . .

CLERK: Oh, I see, you don't have a dear departed, you just want to buy a grave plot.

BETH: Yes, that's right.

CLERK: Right, then we won't need the blue form for the gravediggers, just a straightforward sale docket.

The CLERK *writes details on a form,* BETH *watches nervously.*

BETH: It's my mother . . . she's . . . she's terminally ill . . . she insisted that I buy a grave now . . . .

CLERK: She wants to know where she's going to lie . . .

BETH: Yes, that's exactly what she said . .

CLERK: That's very responsible of her. The older generation are more sensible about these things.

BETH: We have a family plot in the old cemetery, but it's full.

CLERK: Yes, they all are. The new cemetery's very nice though. The council are always being complimented on the flowering shrubs . . . something in bloom all the year round . . . does your mother like flowers?

BETH (*slightly startled*): Yes, yes she does actually.

CLERK (*pleased*): Well, there you are then.

BETH: Would it be possible to have a plot near the old cemetery wall . . . she wants to be as near her mother and father as possible . . .

CLERK: Ah now, that depends . . .

BETH: On what?

CLERK: On whether you want a Protestant or a Catholic plot.

BETH: You're joking.

CLERK: Indeed not. The new cemetery is divided in two by a gravel path. Protestant graves are to the right, Catholic graves to the left. Now what side would your mother want?

BETH: The right, definitely the right.

CLERK: Ah good, you're in luck, the Protestant graves go right up to the old cemetery wall . . . now let me see . . . I can offer you a choice of two . . .

The CLERK *shows* BETH *the plan of the cemetery.* BETH *looks at it and then hands it back to the* CLERK.

BETH: I can't . . . I just can't . . . you pick one for me.

CLERK: There's a lovely hydrangea behind this one . . .

BETH: That'll do . . .

CLERK: Or this one has a forsythia . . . absolutely laden with yellow blossoms in the spring . . .

BETH: The hydrangea will do nicely, thank you.

CLERK: Yes, you're probably right, they have a much longer flowering period . . . now if you'll just sign here.

BETH *signs the docket.*

CLERK: And your address here . . . You know, I wish there were more people like your mother.

BETH: Dying?

CLERK: Oh no no . . . organised . . . buying their final resting place in advance of the event. It saves the relative a lot of trouble when the call comes from above, makes it easier to organise the funeral. You've no idea how difficult it all is, if people go and die at the weekend and the family has no burial plot.

BETH: I suppose you own a grave plot.

CLERK: Oh indeed, yes, in the old cemetery. I bought one years ago when I saw how quickly it was filling up . . .

(She leans forward and speaks confidentially in hushed tones to BETH.*)* Laid my Jack to rest there the year before last . . . my husband . . . cancer . . . very nasty . . .

BETH: Yes it is.

CLERK: Your mother? . . . Same thing?

BETH: Yes.

The CLERK *pats* BETH's *hand.*

CLERK: I hope she doesn't linger too long.

BETH *pulls her hand away, angrily.*

BETH: Oh, I do.

CLERK: Oh no, my dear, take it from one who's been through it . . . You won't want her to linger . . . my Jack lingered . . . very nasty when they linger, for them and for you . . . is your mother in the hospital?

BETH: No, she's in my house.

CLERK: A little bit of advice, dear . . . at the end . . . don't let them take her into the hospital . . . all they do is drag it out . . .

BETH: I really must go, I don't like leaving her alone for too long . . .

CLERK: Now this is only a sales docket. I'll post you out the deeds to the bit of ground sometime next week, all right? That will be fifty pounds, dear, just make the cheque payable to the North Down District Council.

The CLERK *compares the cheque with the cheque card.*

BETH: Tell me something . . . why is the new cemetery segregated? The old one wasn't, was it?

CLERK: Not officially, but the people sort of segregated it themselves. If you walk around the old cemetery you'll see what I mean. There's clumps of Catholics and clumps of Protestants. The odd one buried among the wrong crowd stands out like a sore thumb.

BETH: So the council decided to make it

official in the new cemetery?

CLERK: They did, makes it easier for everybody.

BETH: What happens in a mixed marriage . . . do you bury them under the gravel path?

The CLERK *is not at all amused by this sort of levity.* ·

BETH: Sorry . . . it was only a joke . . .

CLERK: Is your family mixed . . . will the segregation bother your mother?

BETH: Bother my mother? . . . She'll be tickled pink when I tell her.

BETH *moves out of the council office to the street outside. She takes a deep breath, relieved that the episode is over.* THERESA *approaches.* BETH *doesn't see her.*

THERESA: Excuse me, missus, could you direct me to Sandy Row? I've a date with a big sexy Orangeman.

BETH: Theresa . . . I thought you weren't coming home from London till next weekend.

THERESA: I said I'd *see* you next weekend. I'm going to Dublin this week for our Danny's wedding. Pay attention when you're reading my letters.

BETH: I forgot . . . God, I'm so confused . . .

THERESA: So what else is new? Beth, are you all right? . . . You look . . . strange. What were you doing in there?

BETH: You'd never believe me if I told you. Theresa, come and see me as soon as you get back to Belfast . . . I need to talk to you.

THERESA: Let's go and get a cup of coffee and talk now.

BETH: I can't . . . I've got to get back to my mother.

THERESA: How is she?

BETH: Surviving . . . Theresa, I'm sorry . . . I'll have to go. I'll see you soon.

THERESA: I'll phone you the minute I get back. Give my love to your mother.

BETH *walks to where* SARAH *lies on the sofa.*

BETH: You promised to stay in bed till I got back.

SARAH: The bands have been out practisin' for the Twelfth, came right past the house, so they did. You should have heard those boyos play.

BETH: You could have fallen.

SARAH: I took it slowly.

BETH: You've exhausted yourself, your face is all flushed.

SARAH: It's the sound of the flute bands . . . always gets the oul Protestant blood going. I tell you, a daily dose of the True Blue Defenders would do me more good than them hateful transfusions they give me up at the hospital . . . how long is it now till the Twelfth?

BETH: Ten days.

SARAH: I'll see it one more time before I go, if God spares me.

BETH: You'll have a ringside seat at that window.

SARAH: If I'm well enough on the day will you take me down to the end of the driveway in the car? I want to sit with the windows rolled down and be a proper part of it one last time.

BETH: It's a wonder you don't want me to drive you to the Field at Finaghy.

SARAH: If I thought I could manage it, I would. But sure what's the point of kiddin' myself. I'll be lucky if I can make it to the gate, even in the car.

BETH: You'll make it.

SARAH: God willing . . . Did you get that wee bit of business done for me?

BETH: Yes.

SARAH: And were you able to get a plot near the old cemetery?

BETH: Right at the wall . . . do you

know if you'd been a Catholic, you'd have been out of luck.

SARAH: How do you mean?

BETH: The new cemetery is segregated. Prods to the right, Fenians to the left. The Protestant graves are alongside the old cemetery.

SARAH finds this very funny. She laughs delightedly.

SARAH: God, isn't is great to know that you'll be lying among your own.

BETH's face contorts and she turns her head away.

SARAH: Ach now, child, I didn't mean to upset you . . . don't look like that. You have to face up to these things. I'm sorry I had to ask you to go to that place for me, if I'd been fit enough I would have gone myself.

BETH: I'm all right, honestly, I'm all right.

SARAH: And now my mind's at rest knowing it's done and we don't need to think about it or talk about it any more . . . I think I'll go back to bed for a wee while . . . hearing the oul bands has took more out of me than I thought.

BETH: Would you like a cup of tea?

SARAH: I would love a cup of tea.

BETH and SARAH (*together*): In a china cup.

They both laugh. BETH helps SARAH to her feet.

SARAH: You're a good child. I don't know what I'd do without you.

BETH: What am *I* going to do without *you*?

SARAH: Grow up . . . change, the way everybody does when their mother dies . . . now you go and make the tea, I'll go to bed myself.

BETH: I'll help you in first.

SARAH: No, I want to manage myself for as long as I can.

BETH watches SARAH as she walks slowly towards the darkened part of the stage. At the edge of the light SARAH turns around.

SARAH: You know, if I'm well enough on the twelfth of July, we will go to the Field, you and me. I'd like to stand there with you beside me, one more time, just like when you were a child. I carried you to the Field at Finaghy when you were a few months old, do you know that?

BETH (*smiling*): Yes, I know that.

SARAH: You mind it now, you mind all the old family stories, tell them to your children after I'm gone.

SARAH turns and steps into the darkness. BETH makes an involuntary gesture as if to stop her from leaving. BETH walks forward and addresses the audience.

BETH: She carried me to the Field when I was four months old. She was sitting on the grass, her back to a hedge, giving me a bottle, when a gentleman in a clerical collar came up and patted us both on the head. 'I'm proud of you, daughter,' he said to my mother, 'coming all this way with a young baby. Women like you are the backbone of Ulster.' She knew he was a gentleman, because apart from the clerical collar, he had a hard hat and white gloves. The upper-class Orangemen always wear a hard hat and white gloves. She was very proud that a man like that had stopped to pay the likes of her such a compliment. I have an image in my mind of that day . . . the hedge littered with empty bottles and bits of red, white and blue paper, my mother feeding me as she sang along with the Orange bands. I couldn't possibly remember it, I was only an infant, but I've heard that story and all the other family stories so often that I can remember and see clearly things that happened even before I was born . . . like the day my mother's brother Samuel went off to fight for

King and Country.

The centre of the stage lightens to show the home of the grandparents, SAM and ANNIE in the year 1939. An enlarged sepia photo of the grandfather in First World War uniform hangs in an ornate frame on the back wall. The GRANDMOTHER *and* SARAH *(aged about twenty-three) are sitting looking miserable. Offstage an Orange band is playing and people are singing 'On the green grassy slopes of the Boyne, Where King Billy and his men went to war, we will fight for our glorious deliverence . . . Where? . . . on the green grassy slopes of the Boyne.' The* GRANDFATHER *comes dancing in, highly excited.*

GRANDFATHER: Man, they're going to see the lads off in great style, so they are. Are the two of yous not comin' out?

SARAH: Where's my wee Sammy? Where's the chile?

GRANDFATHER: I left him playin' with the childer next door. He's all right, he'll come to no harm. You fuss too much about that wain . . . Women!

GRANDMOTHER: I suppose you think I fuss too much about *our* Samuel?

GRANDFATHER: Our Samuel's not a wain any more, he's one of the King's men now.

GRANDMOTHER: He's still only a child This is all your doin', filling his head full of nonsense about the great times you had with the lads in France during the First World War.

GRANDFATHER: It'll make a man of him.

GRANDMOTHER: He's only eighteen. I want him to grow into a man here, in his own street with his own ones all around him, not in some stinkin' hole in the ground in France among strangers.

GRANDFATHER: I was in the trenches

in France when I was little more than a lad. It never did me no harm.

GRANDMOTHER: Oh aye, I suppose you were born with that bit of shrapnel in your leg.

GRANDFATHER: I'd do it again gladly, if they'd have me, for my King and Country.

GRANDMOTHER: But they won't have you, will they, because your oul chest is still full of gas from the last great war.

She says the word 'Great' with contempt. SARAH *goes and looks outside.*

GRANDFATHER: My son will represent me. You should be proud of him, not sittin' here mopin'.

GRANDMOTHER: You're an oul fool, you always were.

SARAH: He's comin' up the street. Now don't be arguing, you two, you don't want to upset him. God knows when we'll all be together again.

Offstage there is cheering from the crowd. SAMUEL *comes in dressed in Second World War uniform.*

SAMUEL: The band's marching with us to the boat. I've never seen anything like it. It's like the twelfth of July out there.

GRANDFATHER: Don't yous all deserve it? The young men of this road are doing Ulster proud.

GRANDMOTHER: I've made you some sandwiches, son, in case you get hungry.

SAMUEL: Ach mammy, I can't go off to war with a packet of sandwiches in my hand. Do you want me to be a laughin' stock?

GRANDFATHER: Take a bit of advice from an old campaigner, son. Put them sandwiches in your pocket. Army life's grand, but you'll not get the good food you're used to at home.

SAMUEL *puts the sandwiches in his pocket.*

SAMUEL: I'll probably get my pay docked for ruining the line of my uniform.

GRANDMOTHER: The line of your uniform'll be well ruined after a night sleepin' rough in thon oul boat.

Offstage there is more cheering from the crowd.

SAMUEL: I'll have to go. They're lining up . . .

GRANDFATHER: Good luck, son.

SAMUEL: Thanks, father.

They shake hands awkwardly. The GRANDFATHER turns away, overcome with emotion. To hide this, he blows his nose noisily. The GRANDMOTHER embraces her son.

SAMUEL: It won't be for long . . . I'll be back before you know it, with a string of medals on my chest.

GRANDMOTHER: Never you mind the medals, Samuel. You just keep your head down, and come home in one piece.

GRANDFATHER: And go easy on the oul French water son, it's not like the good clean stuff you get here. They're awful clarty people the French . . . Catholics you know . . . .

SARAH *embraces her brother.*

SARAH: Now you take care of yourself, do you hear? No heroics.

SAMUEL: And you take care of mother.

SARAH: I will.

SAMUEL: Where's my namesake?

SARAH: He's next door, playin' . . .

GRANDFATHER: I'll go and get him. He'll have to see his uncle off . . .

As the GRANDFATHER goes out the GRANDMOTHER's sister MAISIE rushes in.

MAISIE: They're linin' up, ready to go. Ach boys a dear, don't you look great . . . how's about a big kiss for your aunt before you get stuck intil them Germans.

She hugs SAMUEL exuberantly.

MAISIE: God bless you, love. You show them Germans what the Ulster Protestant boys are made of. Here's a wee something for you from your aunt Maisie.

She puts some money into his hand. SAMUEL is embarrassed.

SAMUEL: There's no need . . .

MAISIE: You put it in your pocket. Always have a wee roughness of money about you when you're away from home . . . for emergencies.

The GRANDMOTHER removes her wedding ring and places it on SAMUEL's finger.

GRANDMOTHER: Don't take it off, no matter what. It'll guard you, bring you home safe.

SAMUEL *kisses her and moves away. He is close to tears.*

SARAH: Don't forget to write . . .

As he goes out the crowds outside cheer and the band begins to play.

MAISIE: Come on the pair of you, we have to see him off . . .

MAISIE *rushes out.* SARAH *puts her arms around her mother and walks her to the door. The sounds of the bands are replaced by the sounds of war. SARAH comes back on stage reading a letter from SAMUEL. At one side of the stage the lights brighten on SAMUEL. He is in an army billet somewhere in France sitting on the floor, leaning on his kitbag, writing the letter that SARAH is reading. They read the letter together.*

SARAH AND SAMUEL: My darling sister, this is to let you know I have arrived safe and well. We got here late as the boat was held up for days because of fog, and we had our Christmas dinner in the middle of the English Channel. My father was right when he said that the food's not what we're used to at home, but then nobody can cook a dinner like my mother. The drink here is dirt cheap, best rum about 1/6 for a ten-glass bottle. If it was that price at home, the men on our road would never sober up. It's just as well that I don't drink, not that I could afford to set the town on fire even if I wanted to. They only give us thirty francs a week while we're here, that's roughly 3/6. It means that I'm saving about seven bob a week, so that by the time I get leave, I hope round the beginning of June, I'll have a nice wee bit put by to bring home to my mother. The life here is okay. The locals are nice but funny, you know, different from us. We are billeted in an old chapel, which is dry and quite comfortable, although, mind you, I don't think the Pope would be too happy if he got to hear about the Orange Sash rolled up inside my kitbag. I brought it with me for luck. If you see anybody from the lodge, tell them that the Ulster boys in France are thinking about them and I hope they're praying for us when they meet at the Orange Hall. Your loving brother, Samuel.

SARAH *exits reading* SAMUEL's *letter. The sounds of war increase then fade into the sound of a typewriter. A British Army* OFFICER *walks on and faces the audience. He stands very erect, hands behind his back, dictating an official letter to an unseen secretary in the background. The* GRAND-MOTHER *walks on (from where* SARAH *has exited) reading this buff-coloured official communication.*

OFFICER: Form B104 stroke 81 stoke AS. R.A. Records. C.D. and A.A. Branch. Footscray. Sidcup. Kent. Third June 1940. Sir or Madam . . .

GRANDMOTHER: I regret to have to inform you that a report has been received by the War Office to the effect that . . .

OFFICER: Number 1473529 . . .

GRANDMOTHER: Gunner Samuel Bell . . .

OFFICER: Eleven stroke Third Signal Regiment, Royal Artillery. . .

GRANDMOTHER: Has been wounded and was admitted to Saint Luke's Emergency Hospital, Bradford, on the first day of June 1940 . . .

OFFICER: The nature of the wound . . .

GRANDMOTHER: Gunshot wounds in the chest . . .

OFFICER: I am to express to you the sympathy of the Army Council. Any further information received as to his condition will be at once notified to you. Yours faithfully . . .

GRANDMOTHER: Lieutenant Colonel . . . Cromie? . . . Crowe? . . . Croft? . . . Officer in charge of records.

OFFICER: Important! Any change of address should be notified immediately to this office.

The GRANDMOTHER *holds the letter to her face and exits, weeping. As she leaves, the* OFFICER *intones impassively.*

OFFICER: If replying, please quote number ED stroke CAS stroke N.

He exits. BETH *walks on and addresses the audience.*

BETH: My Great Aunt Maisie looked after my brother Sammy while my mother and my grandmother went to Bradford to visit Samuel in St Luke's hospital. I went too, barely formed inside my mother's womb. It was a beautiful day, the day we arrived. The wounded lay on stretchers outside on the grass, their bandages removed. Seemingly, there was some desperate hope that exposure to the sun's rays could stop the spread of gangrene. The smell was indescribable. Luckily the weather turned cold, so the doomed soldiers were allowed indoors to die. We stayed for two weeks, and Samuel, although he didn't get any better, at least appeared not to get any worse. As soon as we got back to Belfast, my Great Aunt Maisie took my grandmother to consult a fortune teller.

The stage lightens on the FORTUNE TELLER. *The* GRANDMOTHER *is sitting facing her.* SARAH *and* MAISIE *watch and listen.*

FORTUNE TELLER: You must cross my palm with silver, for luck.

The GRANDMOTHER *puts a coin into the* FORTUNE TELLER's *hand. She holds out her hand for more, the* GRANDMOTHER *gives it, the* FORTUNE TELLER *pockets the coins.*

SARAH: She's worse than the money lender.

MAISIE: She's worth every penny, listen.

FORTUNE TELLER: You have great trouble, great sorrow . . .

GRANDMOTHER: Yes.

FORTUNE TELLER: Somebody you love is very ill . . .

GRANDMOTHER: Yes.

FORTUNE TELLER: I see soldiers . . . running . . . falling . . . guns firing . . . not here, on foreign soil.

GRANDMOTHER: France.

FORTUNE TELLER: A young man is wounded . . . an artillery gunner . . . dark haired . . . very young . . . your son . . .

MAISIE (*to* SARAH): Didn't I tell you she was good?

SARAH: She could have got all that from the paper. There was a photo of Samuel along with the write-up about him being wounded.

MAISIE: I'm telling you, she has the gift.

SARAH: Aye, of the gab . . .

FORTUNE TELLER (*angrily*): Shush!

MAISIE: Sorry missus.

GRANDMOTHER: Can you see into the future as well as the past?

FORTUNE TELLER: What is it you want to know?

GRANDMOTHER: My son that's wounded . . . will he be all right?

FORTUNE TELLER: He'll come home to you.

GRANDMOTHER: Are you sure?

FORTUNE TELLER: I'm sure your son will return to Belfast from Bradford.

MAISIE: Now how did she know that eh? There was no mention of Bradford in the paper.

SARAH: She could have heard about it on the road. Everybody knows we were in Bradford.

GRANDMOTHER: God bless you missus.

The FORTUNE TELLER *nods impassively. The* GRANDMOTHER *gets to her feet. She is very emotional.* MAISIE *goes to her puts her arm around her and leads her off.* SARAH *looks at the* FORTUNE TELLER *sceptically and turns to follow them.*

FORTUNE TELLER: Wait . . . I want to have a word with you . . . sit down.

SARAH *sits down slowly, warily.*

FORTUNE TELLER: You're her daughter?

SARAH: Yes.

FORTUNE TELLER: Do you live with her?

SARAH: I thought you knew everything.

FORTUNE TELLER (*coldly*): Make sure your mother isn't alone at any time over the next few days. She'll be getting the telegram.

SARAH: But you said . . . you told her he'd come home . . .

FORTUNE TELLER: An Army coffin is what he's comin' home in.

SARAH: You're an evil old woman!!

FORTUNE TELLER: I don't decide what happens, I only see.

SARAH: You see nothin' you make it up as you go along . . . or you tell gullible people what any fool with ears and eyes could hear on the road or read in the papers.

FORTUNE TELLER: He's dyin' . . . he won't last the week.

SARAH: You're a liar . . . you're a fake . . . you do it for the money . . . you take money from poor desperate people and tell them . . . tell them . . . I don't believe you . . . he won't die . . . you know nothin' . . . nothin' . . .

Distraught, SARAH *is now standing accusing the* FORTUNE TELLER, *who remains impassive, cold.*

FORTUNE TELLER: Give me your hand.

SARAH *stares at her as if mesmerised.*

FORTUNE TELLER: Sit down and give me your hand.

SARAH *sits down slowly and stares at the* FORTUNE TELLER. *The* FORTUNE TELLER *holds out her hand and* SARAH *slowly places her hand on top.*

FORTUNE TELLER: You have a three-year-old son. He has the same name as the wounded soldier.

SARAH: That's common knowledge.

FORTUNE TELLER: You're expecting again . . . is that common knowledge?

SARAH, *startled, looks down at her abdomen.*

FORTUNE TELLER: It doesn't show. I can see the two heartbeats.

SARAH: I've only just missed a month.

FORTUNE TELLER: And you've told nobody, not even that waster you married . . . so you can't say I heard about that on the road, or read it in the papers.

SARAH: Please . . . please . . . tell me he's not going to die.

FORTUNE TELLER: I told you, I don't decide, I only see.

SARAH *gets wearily to her feet. The* FORTUNE TELLER *holds out her hand.* SARAH *gives her a silver coin. The* FORTUNE TELLER *still holds out her hand.*

SARAH: I don't have any more.

FORTUNE TELLER: Lost it all on the horses again, did he?

SARAH: The dog track.

She walks away. The FORTUNE TELLER *pockets the coin and shrugs. She calls after* SARAH.

FORTUNE TELLER: And it'll be a girl . . . and neither of yous will have your sorrows to seek . . .

The lights darken around her, and lighten on the other side of the stage to show the Army OFFICER *reciting the telegram. As he reads, the centre of the stage lightens to show the* GRANDFATHER *hanging an enlarged tinted photo of* SAMUEL *in Second World War uniform beside the sepia photo of himself in First World War uniform. The* GRANDMOTHER *sits listening as* SARAH *reads the newspaper report of* SAMUEL's *death.*

OFFICER: Deeply regret to inform you 1473529 Samuel Bell, 113 Signal Regiment died from gunshot wounds 17.40 hours. R.A. Records.

SARAH: Death of Belfast Gunner . . . Result of war wounds . . . Prominent in Orange Order . . . Gunner Samuel Bell . . . son of . . . son of . . . Gunner Bell was with the B.E.F. at Dunkirk . . . A prominent figure in the Orange and Black Orders, he personified the bravery and loyalty of the sons of Ulster . . . four of his cousins are at present serving their country overseas . . . his father served with the Royal Ulster Rifles in the last great war . . . there's a photo with his name underneath . . .

GRANDMOTHER: Cut it out, I'll put it away with the telegram and the letters.

GRANDFATHER: There'll be money to come, you know . . .

The GRANDMOTHER *looks at him with contempt.*

GRANDFATHER: I'm only sayin' . . . we're entitled . . .

The GRANDMOTHER *continues to stare at him silently.*

GRANDFATHER: I'm only sayin' . . .

SARAH: Father, just leave it . . . leave it.

The GRANDMOTHER *takes some money from her purse and hands it to the* GRANDFATHER.

GRANDMOTHER: Here, away down to the pub and give my head peace.

The GRANDFATHER *takes the money. He looks as if he wants to say something but is put off by his wife's cold stare. He walks to the door and turns.*

GRANDFATHER: He was my son too, you know.

The lights darken on the centre of the stage and lighten on BETH *at one side. She addresses the audience.*

BETH: Eventually the Army sorted out how much Samuel had saved while he was in France. They added up all the seven shillingses and deducted an amount to cover the cost of the kit he'd lost on the beaches of Dunkirk. There was no pension. He was not considered old enough to have any dependent relatives. The Army did provide, free of charge, a war grave in a Belfast cemetery. My grandmother scrubbed boards in a bakery to pay for the white marble headstone and surround. For the rest of her life she forbade her family to buy anything that was German made. After the war, an American cousin married a German. As far as my grandmother was concerned, that particular branch of the family tree ceased to exist.

The lights rise on the GRAND-PARENTS *house in March 1941.* SARAH, *very pregnant, is saying goodbye to her* MOTHER.

GRANDMOTHER: Now you put your feet up when you get home, Sarah, you're done in. Let your man put the wee lad to bed.

SARAH: I'll see you tomorrow.

GRANDMOTHER: I'll come and see you tomorrow, save you walkin' round.

SARAH: All right.

They embrace and SARAH *walks towards the door.*

GRANDMOTHER: Sarah?

SARAH: What?

GRANDMOTHER: Is everything all right at home?

SARAH: Yes, everything's all right.

GRANDMOTHER: I'll see you tomorrow then.

SARAH: See you tomorrow.

As she reaches the door, SARAH *suddenly doubles forward.*

SARAH: Oh, dear God.

GRANDMOTHER: What is it?

SARAH: Oh no, I think I'm startin' . . . oh dear God . . .

GRANDMOTHER: Come in and shut that door, don't be makin' an exhibition of yourself in front of the neighbours. Come back and sit down for a minute, it might be a false alarm, you remember the way you were with Sammy . . . stoppin' and startin'.

As she is talking she gets SARAH *to the chair. Immediately there is another contraction, and* SARAH *gasps with the pain.*

SARAH: I can feel the child movin' down.

GRANDMOTHER: We'd better get you to the hospital. Now don't you move, I'll get our Maisie.

SARAH *yells as wave after wave of pain engulfs her.*

SARAH: There's something wrong . . . it doesn't feel right . . .

GRANDMOTHER: You can't go on the bus in that state . . . I'll run to the shop and ask them to phone for a taxi.

SARAH: I've no money for a taxi . . . I've no money for anything . . . he hasn't been home for two days . . . not since he lifted his wages . . .

GRANDMOTHER: Gods curse him . . . I'll get the money somewhere . . . you hold on . . . Maisie'll know what to do . . . keep your knees together till I get back . . .

She rushes out. The lights darken. BETH addresses the audience.

BETH: I was born breech on March the eighth, a jaundiced, sickly, underweight child. My mother was advised by the ward sister to take me home and love me, because I was delicate and probably wouldn't last long. She was also advised by the Grand Master of the local Orange Lodge that I wouldn't die as the eighth of March was the anniversary of the death of William, Prince of Orange, and this was a good omen. God works in mysterious ways and, as he and King Billy had obviously sent me as a replacement for my heroic Uncle Samuel, I should be called Mary after the Good King's wife. I didn't die, but I wasn't called Mary either. It's a very Catholic sort of name in Northern Ireland, despite King Billy's wife, and my mother didn't fancy it at all. She compromised by calling me Elizabeth, after the heir to the throne.

July 1952. Sounds of Orange bands playing 'The Sash My Father Wore'. The GRANDMOTHER, MAISIE and BETH as a child of eleven come dancing into the GRANDMOTHER's house, singing and giggling. They all fall laughing on to the sofa. SARAH comes in from the other side

of the stage carrying a tray of tea in china cups.

SARAH: Beth, look at the state of you, your face is black.

GRANDMOTHER: Ach, leave the child alone, you can't expect her to be neat and tidy all the time.

SARAH: She looks like one of them wee street urchins from the Catholic quarter.

MAISIE *spits on a handkerchief and cleans BETH's face, BETH finds this unpleasant and struggles.*

GRANDMOTHER: Is Sammy still sleepin'?

SARAH: He is, he must be sickenin' for somethin'. His face is awful hot.

MAISIE (*to* BETH): Keep still, child . . . there now, that's a bit more Protestant-lookin'.

BETH: Are all the Catholic children dirty?

MAISIE: I never seen a clean one yet.

BETH: Why are they dirty?

GRANDMOTHER: It's just the way they are. They're not like us.

MAISIE: They never scrub their front steps nor black-lead their fires nor nothin'. They're clarty and poor.

BETH: Are we not poor?

GRANDMOTHER: There's poor and poor. We keep our houses nice, always dress clean and respectable. There's no shame in a neat darn or a patch as long as a body is well washed.

MAISIE: And we don't go about cryin' poverty and puttin' a poor mouth on ourselves the way they do neither. Did you hear thon oul nationalist politician on the wireless the other day? Tellin' the world about goin' to school bare-fut in his da's cut-down trousers? I would cut my tongue out before I'd demean my family like that.

BETH: Mammy made this dress out of one of her old skirts.

SARAH: Don't you ever go sayin' that to strangers.

BETH: Why?

SARAH: Because you just don't, that's why. I don't know where I got her at all. She hasn't the sense she was born with.

GRANDMOTHER: Why don't you go and lie down, Sarah, you look awful tired.

SARAH: I've had no sleep for two nights with our Sammy, up and down gettin' drinks of water. I think it must be the flu he has.

GRANDMOTHER: Away upstairs and take the weight off your feet for an hour or two. Sure the men won't be back till the pubs close.

SARAH: I think I will. Now you behave yourself, Beth, and give your granny and Aunt Maisie peace.

She goes out. The GRANDMOTHER *and* MAISIE *sip their tea contentedly.* BETH *sits looking miserable.*

MAISIE: There's nothin' like a drop of tea in a china cup . . . what's up with her? (*Nodding towards* BETH.)

GRANDMOTHER: I don't know. What's wrong, child?

BETH: When I want a drink of water in the night she shouts at me, she never shouts at our Sammy.

GRANDMOTHER: You're easily bothered.

MAISIE: Is that all?

BETH: I don't see why my mammy was so annoyed with me. I like this dress.

GRANDMOTHER: Of course you do, it's lovely.

MAISIE: Your mammy was always very clever with a needle and thread, so she was.

BETH: Well, what's wrong with saying she made it out of her old skirt?

GRANDMOTHER: It's all right to say it in front of us, your own family, it's strangers you don't say that sort of thing to.

BETH: Why?

MAISIE: Why? *Why?* I swear to God, that wain was born askin' questions.

GRANDMOTHER: Because it's family business and it's private. No matter how hard times are, you don't let yourself down in front of the neighbours.

MAISIE: Because if you do, you bring yourself down to the level of the Catholics, whining and complainin' and puttin' a poor mouth on yourself.

GRANDMOTHER: No matter how poor we are, child, we work hard and keep ourselves and our homes clean and respectable, and we always have a bit of fine bone china and good table linen by us.

MAISIE: If the new Queen herself, God bless her, was to call here for her tea, we could do her proud. None of your old dirt here.

BETH: Mammy had to sell our china cabinet to pay the rentman.

The GRANDMOTHER *and* MAISIE *look at each other. This is obviously news to them.*

GRANDMOTHER: Who did she sell it to?

BETH: Mrs Duffy, Theresa's mammy.

GRANDMOTHER: And all the stuff in it?

BETH: Yes . . . except for one china cup and saucer. She took that out before Mrs Duffy came, and afterwards she made herself a cup of tea in it and she cried and she said she'd never forgive my daddy as long as she lived.

GRANDMOTHER: That child sees and hears more than's good for her.

MAISIE: A fine state of affairs when a God-fearin' hard-working Protestant has to sell her good china to a Fenian to make ends meet.

GRANDMOTHER: Don't you ever go tellin' all that to anybody else, do you hear me, Beth?

BETH: Yes, granny.

The lights darken on this scene. At one side of the stage we see THERESA DUFFY, *a child of eleven, skipping. She sings 'On the hill there stands a lady, who she is I do not know, all she wants is gold and silver, all she wants is a nice young man'.* BETH *arrives and they skip together and sing the song again. They sit down, breathlessly.*

BETH: Theresa?

THERESA: What?

BETH: You know the way your mammy bought my mammy's china cabinet and all the stuff in it?

THERESA: Yes.

BETH: Well, sure you won't tell anybody about it?

THERESA: Why not?

BETH: Because it's private and my granny says nobody's to know.

THERESA: All right . . . I think it's rotten-looking anyway.

BETH: My mammy loved it. She used to polish it every day.

THERESA: My daddy says it's daft having all those cups and saucers and things just for looking at.

BETH: That's what my daddy said too.

THERESA: Have you got your new uniform for the grammar school yet?

BETH: Not yet, my mammy's still saving up to pay for it.

THERESA: I got mine last week. You want to see it. Everything's dark green, even the knickers.

BETH: Our uniform's navy blue.

THERESA: Are the knickers navy blue too?

BETH: Yes.

THERESA: Do you know what that big lad down the street says those sort of knickers are called?

BETH: What?

THERESA: Passion killers.

BETH: What does that mean?

THERESA: I don't know. I asked my mammy and she hit me and made me go to confession.

They sit and ponder this for a moment.

BETH: Aren't your teachers all nuns?

THERESA: Some of them are. They'll all be nuns when I go to the convent grammar school.

BETH: Is it true that they always go around in pairs because one of them's really a man?

THERESA: Who told you that?

BETH: My Great Aunt Maisie.

THERESA: Nuns are women. The men are called monks. Your aunt's having you on.

BETH: She read it in a book that was written by a girl who escaped from a convent.

THERESA: My granny has a book about a rich Protestant landowner, and all these young Catholic girls worked in his big house and they all got babies, so they did.

BETH: Were they married?

THERESA: No, they weren't.

BETH: Your granny's head's cut. You have to be married to get a baby.

THERESA: I have a cousin who's not married and she got a baby.

BETH: How?

THERESA: I don't know. I asked my mammy about that too, and she hit me again.

The lights darken on the two puzzled children. BETH *as an adult addresses the audience.*

BETH: We knew nothing. We found it impossible to get an accurate answer to anything relating to bodily functions. Babies were a gift from God to married women. I asked my Great Aunt Maisie why God gives more gifts to the Catholics if the Protestants of Ulster were his chosen people. She said it was because the Catholics were greedy. They were always looking for something for nothing. My mother did attempt to have a serious talk with me once. It was very confusing and embarrassing for both of us.

At the other side of the stage BETH aged eleven is sitting in a chair reading a comic. SARAH is ironing, her back is to BETH.

SARAH: Beth?

BETH: What?

SARAH: Don't say what, say pardon.

BETH: Pardon.

SARAH; That's better . . . I want to explain something to you . . . you're growing up and there's things you have to be told . . . are you listening?

Embarrassed, she keeps her back firmly to BETH.

BETH: Yes, mammy.

SARAH: Some time . . . in the next year or two . . . there's a thing that happens to girls of your age . . . it happens once a month . . . you know where you go to the toilet . . . down there . . .

BETH: Yes.

SARAH: Well, once a month . . . when you start to grow up . . . to become a young woman . . . you get . . . you get . . . a drop of blood comes out of there . . .

BETH (*startled*): Blood?

SARAH: Now there's nothing to worry about. It happens to all women . . . it's just a part of growing up . . . it doesn't do you any harm . . . it comes for a few days and then it goes

away again . . . until the next month. When it happens, you tell me, you don't go telling your father or our Sammy, do you hear?

BETH: Do my daddy and Sammy not know about it?

SARAH: You don't talk to men about that sort of thing, it's not nice.

BETH: Why does it happen . . . what's it for?

SARAH: It's just one of those things women have to put up with . . . there's a lot of things in life that women have to put up with, you'll find that out as you get older . . . and another thing, Beth, when you do get older and maybe go out with boys . . . don't ever let them do anything that's not nice . . . always remember, your private parts are your own . . . do you understand that now?

BETH (*uncertainly*): Yes mammy.

SARAH: That's a good girl.

Relieved that the talk is over, SARAH folds up the ironing board and carries it off without looking at BETH. BETH sits with a puzzled look on her face. She looks down at herself, shrugs and continues reading her comic. Lights darken on BETH. At the other side of the stage the eleven-year-old THERESA appears in green convent uniform. She is carrying a schoolbag. She waves and calls towards the darkened part of the stage.

THERESA: Beth! Beth!

BETH steps into the light. She is not in a uniform, just a dress and cardigan. She also is carrying a schoolbag.

THERESA: Mine started, last night, just when I was getting ready for bed.

BETH: Now we're both grown up.

THERESA: Yes.

BETH: Did your mammy cry?

THERESA: No. But she told me I wasn't to wash my hair while I had it or put

my feet in cold water, or the blood
would all rush to my head and I'd die.
Did your mammy cry?

BETH: A wee bit. She said, 'God help
you child, this is the start of all your
troubles.'

THERESA: My mammy calls it the curse.

BETH: I wish somebody would tell us
what it's all about. I mean, if it's going
to bring us some sort of trouble, do
you not think we should know?

THERESA: Sure they never tell you anything.

BETH: I like your uniform. It's lovely.

THERESA: Why are you not going to the
grammar school, Beth?

BETH: My mammy can't afford the
uniform, but don't be telling anybody,
because I'm not allowed to say.

THERESA: All right.

*They walk off together. The stage
lightens on the* GRANDMOTHER's
house, where SARAH, MAISIE *and
the* GRANDMOTHER *are talking.*

GRANDMOTHER: You should have let
me buy the uniform, Sarah. It's a cryin'
shame, a clever child like that missin'
her chance.

SARAH: It's not just the uniform, it's all
the other expenses over the years . . .
books, games equipment, trips, extras
. . . I can't depend on him for the
money. At least at the secondary
school she'll be as good as the rest of
them, better even because she's so
bright, in the grammar school she'd
have been like a poor relation.

MAISIE: You can get help with the
uniform you know.

SARAH: I'm not runnin' to the assistance
pleadin' poverty.

GRANDMOTHER: It's a disgrace. If they
pass the exam the government should
pay for the lot, not expect workin'
people to fork out for the extras.

MAISIE: They say this Butler Education Act is a great thing for the
workin'-class children. Me eye it is.
What I want to know is why kids like
Theresa Duffy can get their fees paid
to go to a Fenian grammar school, and
one of ours has to miss out.

SARAH: The Duffys have always had a
wee roughness of money about them
. . . and I don't begrudge Theresa her
chance, she passed the exam, she
deserves it.

MAISIE: Not as much as our Beth she
doesn't. No good'll come of this
subsidised education, you mark my
words. The Catholics will beg, borrow
and steal the money to get their kids
a fancy education. This country'll
suffer for it in years to come when
well-qualified Catholics start to pour
out of our Queen's University expecting
the top jobs, wantin' a say in the
runnin' of the country.

She points to SAMUEL's *photo.*

MAISIE: Is that what him and all the
others died for, eh? To educate the
Catholics so that they can take over
Ulster? By God he's well out of it. He
must be turnin' in his grave this day.

GRANDMOTHER: He'd be thirty now if
he'd lived. Sometimes I try to picture
him as a man, married maybe, with a
family of his own, but I can only see
him as a lad of nineteen.

MAISIE: He never needed any woman
while he had you two. He always said
he'd never marry.

GRANDMOTHER: Ach, they all say that
when they're young.

BETH (*to audience*): He remained in their
hearts forever young, forever true, a
perfect son and brother, a perfect
man. If he had survived the war, I
wonder would he have lived up to all
their expectations. No one will ever
know. Perhaps the Germans, without
realising it, killed the only truly honest
Ulsterman who ever lived.

ACT TWO

Offstage, sounds of Orange bands.
SARAH *lies on the velvet sofa in* BETH's
house enjoying the sights and sounds.
BETH *comes in with a tray of tea.*
The music dies away.

SARAH: Only five more days till the
twelfth.

BETH: If they have any more practice
runs, they'll be worn out before the
actual event.

SARAH: Not at all. They get better every
day.

BETH *blows her nose.*

BETH: I don't think my nose is ever
going to stop streaming.

SARAH: Summer colds are always the
worst to shift. Did you put a drop of
butter on the bridge of your nose like
I told you.

BETH: No, I did not.

SARAH: Well, you've only yourself to
blame then.

BETH: My skin's greasy enough without
putting butter on it.

SARAH: Just a wee drop, between the
eyes, and I'm tellin' you, this time
tomorrow your cold'll be gone.

BETH: Old wives' tales.

SARAH: They work. Butter for colds and
burns, everybody knows that.

BETH: A penny on the forehead for
nosebleeds, docken leaves for nettle
stings, a wedding ring to charm away
warts . . .

SARAH: Don't scoff at the old remedies.
Without them you wouldn't have
survived your first year.

BETH: Drink your tea, it'll get cold.

She addresses the audience.

I took whooping cough when I was
eight months old. My grandmother
wrapped me in a blanket and carried
me to the gas-works, where she held
me over the waste gas outlet until I'd
choked and spluttered and coughed up
all the infection. It's one of the family
legends, how I was at death's door
until the Belfast Corporation Gasworks
saved my life.

SARAH: I'm tellin' you, if it wasn't for
the Belfast Corporation Gasworks
you'd be dead . . . I wonder could they
do anything for me? . . . Ach child,
don't look away like that, you have to
face death.

BETH: I can't . . .

SARAH: You must . . . you'll do things
proper for me, won't you?

BETH: You know I will.

SARAH: Promise.

BETH: I promise.

SARAH: With a proper sit-down tea
afterwards.

BETH: With a proper sit-down tea . . .
afterwards.

SARAH: It's a pity your granny and your
Aunt Maisie are gone, they knew the
right way of these things.

BETH: Well, they'd plenty of practice,
hadn't they?

SARAH: Aye, they did that . . . do you
remember the day oul Granda Jamison
died?

BETH: I'll never forget it as long as I
live.

SARAH: It was your own fault. Aunt
Maisie and my mother warned you
you'd be scared, but you insisted on
goin' with them.

BETH: I wasn't scared at the beginning,
just curious to find out why they were
always sent for when somebody in the
street died.

SARAH *laughs.*

SARAH: Well, you found out that day
and no mistake.

There is the sound of bands offstage.
SARAH *looks out the window again.*
The lights darken around BETH's
house and lighten on the other side of
*the stage. A dead man (*GRANDA
JAMISON) *lies on a bed. Offstage the*
bands are still playing. As the sounds
of the bands recede, MAISIE *and*
GRANDMOTHER *come in, followed*
by the child BETH. BETH *looks*
apprehensive. The GRANDMOTHER
looks at her and grins at MAISIE.

GRANDMOTHER: Now are you sure
you want to stay Beth, you can still
change your mind . . .

BETH: I want to stay.

GRANDMOTHER: Well, on your own
head be it now.

MAISIE: She looks a bit green round the
gills to me.

BETH: I'm not.

GRANDMOTHER: You never know,
Maisie, she might have a taste for it.
Maybe after you're gone, she'll take
over and lay out the dead in this street.

MAISIE: The young ones have no
stomach for it.

GRANDMOTHER: You never know, it
could be in her blood, like you and old
Aunt Sarah before you.

MAISIE *goes over to the corpse.*
BETH *stays close to her* GRAND-
MOTHER, *who is taking white*
starched linen covers out of a bag.

MAISIE (*to corpse*): So, you're dead at
last, you oul bugger. By God, there'll
be a quare wake on the road this night.

GRANDMOTHER: Typical of him to die
on the twelfth.

MAISIE: He done it on purpose. Sure he
always took a great delight in being
as much trouble as he could.

The GRANDMOTHER *is covering*
mirrors with the white covers.

BETH: Why are you doing that, granny?

GRANDMOTHER: You must always
cover the mirrors when somebody
dies, or their soul can be reflected
away by evil spirits.

MAISIE: A bit late in the day for him. I
reckon oul Granda Jamison's soul was
took away by evil spirits the day he
was born.

GRANDMOTHER: Aye, you could be
right, but we'll give him the benefit
of the doubt, just in case.

BETH: Was he a bad man?

MAISIE: He was a vindictive oul bastard
all his life, treated his wife and childer
like dogs, so he did.

MRS JAMISON *comes in with a tray*
of tea. She hands it to the GRAND-
MOTHER *and goes over to the corpse*
and looks at him.

MRS JAMISON: All the same, Maisie,
he looks quare and well, doesn't he?

MAISIE: He does indeed, Mrs Jamison,
he does indeed.

She makes a face at the GRAND-
MOTHER *behind* MRS JAMISON's
back. MRS JAMISON *stands looking*
tearfully at the corpse.

MAISIE: Now you go on downstairs, Mrs
Jamison, we'll call you when he's
nicely laid out.

She steers MRS JAMISON *firmly to-*
wards the door. MRS JAMISON *turns*
and looks back at the corpse.

MRS JAMISON: I'll miss him so I will . . .

She goes out.

MAISIE (*imitating her*): I'll miss him so I
will . . . like a hole in the head she'll
miss him.

GRANDMOTHER: Ach now, they were
married a long time.

MAISIE: And this is the first good turn
he's done her since the day and hour
they got married.

BETH: What did he do that was bad?

MAISIE: What did he not do. He was the

sort of man that liked nothin' better than annoyin' people. Always lookin' out for somebody he could do a bad turn to.

The GRANDMOTHER *grins, nudges* BETH *and speaks slyly.*

GRANDMOTHER: In his hey-day, one of his favourite tricks was pickin' an argument with somebody and then takin' out a summons against them when they retaliated.

BETH: What's retaliated?

MAISIE: Givin' him a dig in the gub, that's what retaliated is. By God, it was worth every penny of the ten-shillin' fine to see him lyin' on the pavement.

She lifts up the corpse by the hair and speaks with a mixture of fury and glee.

MAISIE: Do you hear me, you skittery ghost? Worth every penny. This time it's you who's gettin' the summons . . . from your maker.

BETH *runs out, panic stricken.* MAISIE *releases the corpse and laughs.*

MAISIE: Take after me and old Aunt Sarah? Some chance. I told you, the young ones have no stomach for it. Come on, Annie, let's get this oul sinner laid out and then we'll go down the road and see the Orangemen.

The lights darken on the death scene and lighten on SARAH *and* BETH *in* BETH'*s house.*

SARAH: It was the biggest wake the road had ever seen. They came from miles around to make sure that oul Granda Jamison was really dead . . . I wonder . . .

BETH: What?

SARAH: I wonder will there be a big turn out for me . . .

BETH: Don't talk like that.

SARAH: Child, I'm not afraid of dying. Don't you understand? I'm tired, I want to go . . . I've wanted to go for a long time now.

BETH: Don't say that.

SARAH: You wouldn't want me to be dreadin' it, would you?

BETH: I want you to fight it . . . for once in your life, put up a fight. Stop accepting that everything awful has to be, that it's all part of some meaningful eternal plan. People who fight live longer.

SARAH: I don't want to live any longer.

BETH: Not even for me?

SARAH: Particularly not for you. You have a husband in America, you should be there with him, not here nursing me.

BETH: You know Stephen doesn't like me going on business trips with him.

SARAH: You spend too much time apart you two . . . is everything all right between the two of you?

BETH: Yes, of course it is.

SARAH: He hasn't written for a while now.

BETH: He's travelling about a lot.

SARAH: Maybe when he gets back you'll think about startin' a family . . . you're thirty, you don't want to leave it too late.

BETH: There's plenty of time.

SARAH: That's my one regret . . .

BETH: What?

SARAH: That I'll not be alive to see my grandchildren makin' their way in the world . . . Still if it's not to be, it's not to be, and I'll watch over you all from heaven.

BETH: If it's okay with you and God, I'd rather you watched over me from a bit nearer at hand.

SARAH: You get more like your Great Aunt Maisie every day.

BETH: Do you want more tea?

SARAH: No, I think I'll have a wee doze.

BETH: Come on, I'll help you intò bed.

SARAH: No, I'll just doze here, it's comfortable and . . .

BETH: And you'll not miss the bands if they come past again.

SARAH: Do you think there'll be bands in heaven?

BETH: I'd say there's a fair chance that my granny and Aunt Maisie will have it well organised by now.

SARAH: I'm looking forward to seeing them all again, my mother and father, Aunt Maisie . . . and Samuel . . . most of all, Samuel.

BETH: And what about my father . . . or do you think they didn't let him in?

SARAH: Of course they let him in, what a thing to say. He wasn't a bad man your father, just weak, easily led, he loved us all you know, especially you, you were his pride and joy.

BETH: He'd a funny way of showing it.

SARAH: Now, you mustn't speak ill of the dead, especially your own flesh and blood . . . he could have been worse . . . he never lifted a finger to any of us in his life, he just had a weakness for the drink and the bettin' . . . he couldn't help it, he was only a man, God help him.

BETH: Next thing you'll be saying it was all your fault.

SARAH: I sometimes think if I'd bcen a stronger sort of person, you know, took him in hand a bit more, that he'd of turned out all right. I was always too soft.

BETH: You *do* blame yourself.

SARAH: A bit . . . mostly I blame his mother and his sisters for the way they spoilt him . . . What are you smiling at?

BETH: You, and all the other women like you. No matter what a man does wrong it's always some woman's fault, isn't it?

SARAH: Men need lookin's after, like children, sure they never grow up.

BETH: Oh, go to sleep before I lose my temper with you.

She kisses SARAH *and tucks a blanket around her.*

BETH: Did I tell you Theresa's home from London?

SARAH: Is she? Is she coming over to see us?

BETH: Tomorrow.

SARAH: Ach, that'll be nice. I always liked Theresa, a bit flighty maybe, but a good soul at heart.

BETH (*grinning*): Not a bad sort . . . for a Catholic.

SARAH: Like I said, you get more like your Aunt Maisie every day.

Lights darken on BETH *and* SARAH *and lighten on* THERESA *as a girl of eighteen. She is sitting on a chair, waiting to be interviewed for a job in the Northern Ireland Civil Service.* BETH *aged eighteen comes in.*

BETH: Theresa, what are you doing here?

THERESA: Same as you I expect, job interview? God, life's hilarious isn't it? When you think of all the fuss there was about grammar schools and secondary schools, and here we both are, eighteen years old, waiting to be interviewed for boring jobs in the Northern Ireland Civil Service.

BETH: It couldn't be more boring than the job I'm in at the moment. We all sit in rows typing invoices in front of a crabby old man in a glass booth. He taps the window if he sees anyone talking and times us when we go to the toilet.

THERESA: Sounds just like the convent grammar school, only we weren't even lucky enough to have a crabby old man to look at.

BETH: You never liked it, did you?

THERESA: I hated it . . . spent half my time in the sin room.

BETH: The what?

THERESA: The sin room . . . it's where girls got sent for bad behaviour. One of the nuns told me that even when I wasn't behaving immodestly I looked as if I'd like to.

BETH: I wouldn't have thought that there would have been much chance of behaving immodestly in a crowd of girls and nuns.

THERESA: Don't you believe it. They saw sin everywhere. During my life sentence there, they decided that it was unhealthy the way some of the girls walked around the playground with their hands in their skirt pockets. We had to sew the pockets up to remove temptation.

BETH: You're making it up.

THERESA: I am not. They expelled a girl last year for having a dirty book in her locker.

BETH: What dirty book?

THERESA: *The Invisible Man.*

BETH: You'll never last in the Northern Ireland Civil Service, Theresa Duffy, you never take anything seriously.

THERESA: You know, I reckon I've as good as got one of the three jobs that's going here today.

BETH: How do you make that out?

THERESA: Well, I was here early, I've seen all the other candidates going in, and they were all definitely Prods. I'm the only Tague here.

BETH: How would you know what they were?

THERESA: By the look of them. Your eyes are closer set. Did nobody ever tell you that?

BETH: I was always told that the Catholics are the ones with the close-set eyes.

THERESA: Aw don't be telling me that. I've it all worked out. If I'm the only Tague being interviewed, and there are three jobs going, I'm bound to get one of them.

BETH: Why?

THERESA: Why? Because low-grade positions in the Northern Ireland Civil Service are allocated on a strict population basis, two-thirds to the Prods, one-third to the Catholics.

BETH: You're joking again.

THERESA: I'm not. It's to prove to the big wide world that they don't discriminate. Mind you, the Catholic third haven't a hope in hell of being promoted to the top grades. They're allowed so far and then it stops, but at least they employ us.

BETH: The firm I'm with doesn't employ Catholics, at least not in their offices, there are a few in the factory.

THERESA: Aye, and if they could get enough Protestants to fill the factory they'd do that too.

BETH: I'm sorry.

THERESA: Don't be daft, it's nothing to do with you, and anyway, I believe it works the other way round in the South.

BETH: That's not the point, and you live here.

THERESA: Not for long, kid. I'm just going to work here for a while to get some experience, and then I'm off to London.

BETH: London?

THERESA: Aye, London. I'm not stopping here to end up marrying some boozy Catholic layabout who'll give me a baby a year and little else . . . My God, Beth, do you remember all those confused talks we used to have about sex?

BETH: You thought you were pregnant because Joe Maguire put his hand up your skirt.

THERESA: And you told me that I couldn't be pregnant because Joe Maguire had pimples, and boys could only make babies after their spots cleared up. Where did you hear a yarn like that?

BETH: In the school playground, from a wee girl called Iris Agnew.

THERESA: Well, if you ever run into Iris Agnew, you can tell her from me that her theory presented me with a bit of a problem. You see, my da always had spots on his face, they never cleared up, yet my mother kept on producing a baby every other year. I thought she must be an immoral woman who was making babies with somebody else.

BETH: Do you ever wonder what it's like?

THERESA: All the time. When my eldest sister got married, I thought she'd tell me all about it, we were very close.

BETH: And did she not?

THERESA: She came back from the honeymoon with such a stunned look on her face that I hadn't the nerve to ask her . . . Do you ever notice the way women giggle a lot before they're married but they don't giggle much afterwards? I wonder why?

BETH: I suppose we'll find out some-day.

THERESA: That's why I'm going to London . . . to find out without my mother watching me like a hawk. The only way to find out here is to get married, and I'd like to sample it first before I commit myself, just in case it really is a fate worse than death . . . Why don't you come to London with me, and we'll lead a life of delicious sin and debauchery.

BETH: My mother'd never let me go to London. Nobody in our family ever leaves home except to get married.

THERESA: Or to join the British Army.

BETH: The only reason my mother gave in and let our Sammy join the Army was because he couldn't get a decent job here. I think she was worried that if Sammy sat about the house much longer, he'd end up drinking himself to death like my father.

THERESA: I'm sure she misses him.

BETH: Oh yes, you know what my mother's like about Sammy. She consoles herself with the thought that he's learning a good trade.

THERESA: Killing people?

BETH: Motor mechanic.

THERESA: Oh . . . how's he getting on, does he like it?

BETH: He's been posted to Germany. He leaves this afternoon. He can't wait to go. My grandfather says it's only natural, coming from a long line of fighting men the way he does. He was called after an uncle who died in the Second World War, you know.

THERESA: I was called after a saint.

The lights darken on the two girls and lighten on the GRANDMOTHER's *house. The* GRANDFATHER *is hanging a large framed photo of* SAMMY *in Army uniform beside the two photos of himself and* SAMUEL. *The* GRANDMOTHER, MAISIE, SARAH *and* SAMMY *in Army uniform sit drinking tea. The* GRANDFATHER *steps back and looks at the three photos with pride.*

GRANDFATHER: Boys oh dear, isn't that a sight to make a family proud? Three generations for King and Country.

GRANDMOTHER: It's Queen and Country now, you oul fool.

The GRANDFATHER *ignores her and shakes hands with* SAMUEL.

GRANDFATHER: I'm proud of you, lad, proud.

BETH *comes rushing in.*

BETH: Oh, I thought I'd missed you . . .

SARAH: What kept you?

BETH: The interviews ran late, I don't know what the hold-up was.

GRANDFATHER: Bloody civil servants, probably drinkin' tea. They don't know they're livin' that lot.

SARAH: How did you get on?

BETH: All right, I don't think I did too badly. Theresa was there too.

GRANDMOTHER: Theresa Duffy?

BETH: Yes.

MAISIE: I thought she was goin' to the university.

BETH: She changed her mind.

MAISIE: Isn't it a great state of affairs when the Catholics can pick and choose like the Gentry? I don't know why you knock about with her anyway. Do you not know any Protestant girls?

BETH: I don't knock about with Theresa, in fact today's the first time I've seen her in ages.

MAISIE: Ah, yous were always very pally.

BETH: She's a friend. I like her.

MAISIE: Will you still like her if she gets a cushy job in the civil service and you don't?

BETH: Yes, I will.

MAISIE: You've no sense, you, trustin' the Catholics. They're after all our jobs, they're after takin' over.

A car horn sounds offstage. SAMMY *stands up.*

SAMMY: That's me. Time to go.

The rest of the scene is almost a re-enactment of SAMUEL's *departure for war.*

SAMMY: Cheer up everybody, I've been away before.

GRANDMOTHER: Aye, but this time you're goin' overseas.

SARAH: Here, son, I've made you a few sandwiches. It's a long journey.

SAMMY: Mother, they give us a travel allowance, I don't need sandwiches.

GRANDFATHER: They look after them well in the modern Army. When I was in transit with the regiment, we were lucky to get a drink of water, so we were.

GRANDMOTHER: Don't you start reminiscin' about winnin' World War One, or he'll miss the boat.

She hands SAMMY *some money in an envelope.*

GRANDMOTHER: Here, love, you put that away safe, it's from me and Maisie.

He is embarrassed and is about to protest.

MAISIE: Take it. Always have a wee roughness of money about you when you're away from home, for emergencies.

SAMMY *smiles, accepts the money and embraces* MAISIE *and the* GRANDMOTHER.

GRANDFATHER: Good luck, lad.

SAMMY: Thanks, granda.

They shake hands. The GRAND-FATHER *blows his nose to hide his emotions.* SAMMY *embraces his mother,* SARAH.

SARAH: Now, you take care of yourself, do you hear?

SAMMY: I'll be home on leave in no time at all.

SARAH: Of course you will.

GRANDFATHER: You do us proud, son.

SAMMY: I'll come home with a string of medals on my chest.

They all fall silent and look at SAMMY *and then at the photo of* SAMUEL. *The* GRANDMOTHER *begins to cry.*

GRANDMOTHER: Don't say that, Sammy.

SAMMY: What did I say?

SARAH: Nothin' . . . nothin', son, it's all right.

The car horn hoots offstage again.

SAMMY: I'll have to go . . . goodbye Beth.

BETH: Goodbye big brother, take care.

SAMMY: You take care of mother.

BETH: I will.

SAMMY *leaves.* BETH *calls after him.*

BETH: Don't forget to write . . .

They all wave from the door as the car drives off, then the women sit down in silence. The GRANDFATHER *looks proudly at the photos.*

GRANDFATHER: There's no doubt about it, you can't keep a good family down. Another Samuel gone overseas to sort out the Germans.

GRANDMOTHER: He's not away to fight the Germans, he's away to protect them from the Russians. The Germans are our allies now, remember?

GRANDFATHER: Just as long as he doesn't turn his back on them . . .

He stops as he realises what he has said. SARAH *sniffs tearfully. The* GRANDFATHER *looks impatiently at the sad women.*

GRANDFATHER: I'm away to the pub for a bit of cheerful company.

GRANDMOTHER: You're late today. Your oul stomach's probably beginnin' to wonder if your throat's cut.

BETH: I'll walk down the road with you, granda, I'm going to get my hair done.

SARAH: Will you be home for your tea?

BETH: No. Stephen's taking me out for a meal.

She leaves with the GRANDFATHER *and returns to watch (unseen) the three women.*

MAISIE: Is that the Stephen with the car that lives in the big house up the Lisburn Road?

SARAH: It is.

GRANDMOTHER: He's awful well-to-do, Maisie. It could be a quare good match for our Beth, if she plays her cards right.

SARAH: The house belongs to his old aunt, you know. She reared him; his parents died young.

GRANDMOTHER: She has neither chick nor chile of her own. He stands to inherit the lot when she goes.

MAISIE: I hadn't heard him mentioned for a while, I thought it was all off.

SARAH: He's been away in England on business. He goes away a lot on business, but he always gets in touch with our Beth the minute he gets back.

MAISIE: What does he do for a livin'?

SARAH: I'm not sure, but he must make a bit of money at it. He's always well turned out and runs a nice car.

GRANDMOTHER: Tell Maisie about the tea-set, Sarah.

SARAH: Stephen took our Beth up to the house to meet the old aunt, and she stayed for her tea. Our Beth says the house is full of lovely old furniture and good ornaments, and they had their tea out of china that was so fine, our Beth was afraid she'd take a bite out of it.

MAISIE: And why should she feel like that. We've always had a bit of good china about us. Beth's had a cup of tea in a china cup before this.

SARAH: Of course she has, but this was the really old stuff, you know, very very fine.

GRANDMOTHER: Will you tell her about the tea-set.

SARAH: I'm coming to the tea-set . . . after they had their tea the old aunt showed Beth round the house, and apart from all the other nice stuff, do you know what she has?

MAISIE: What?

GRANDMOTHER: A real Belleek tea-set.

SARAH: The real McCoy.

MAISIE: I was never all that struck on Belleek. Do you not think it's awful Fenian-looking'?

SARAH: It's over a hundred years old, it must be worth a fortune.

MAISIE: Oh, I'm sure it is, but I still say you can't beat the fine English bone china.

SARAH: Well, I like it, it's really elegant. The old aunt said it belonged to her grandmother.

GRANDMOTHER: The old aunt has taken a real shine to our Beth from what I can make out.

MAISIE: You'd better start savin', Sarah. It looks as if there might be a weddin' in the offin'.

SARAH: Oh, I started puttin' a bit by for that years ago. When our Beth gets married it's all going to be done proper.

The lights darken on scene and lighten on one side of the stage where BETH *on the eve of her wedding is sitting, looking at herself in the mirror. She lifts a wedding veil and head dress out of a box and sets it on her head. She stares at herself in the mirror. Her expression is sad, pensive. She removes the head dress and puts it back in the box.* THERESA *comes bounding in to the bedroom, singing 'Here Comes the Bride'.* BETH *is delighted to see her.*

BETH: Theresa, when did you get back?

THERESA: This afternoon.

They hug each other delightedly.

The whole road's talking about you. *(She folds her arms over her chest and puts on an exaggerated Belfast accent.)* 'Here, all the same Mrs Jannsen, she's done quare an' well for herself, that wee girl, so she has. A businessman with his own house an' all up the posh end of the Lisburn Road. Fully furnished and wall-to-wall carpet. She'll want for nathin' . . . nathin' . . . '

BETH: You never change, you. I suppose my mother took you on a conducted tour of the wedding presents.

THERESA: As soon as I came in through the door. My God, Beth, you could open a wee shop. How many china tea-sets did you get? I lost count.

BETH: Six.

THERESA: Six? In my flat in London there are five beakers, two of them chipped, and an assortment of plates and bowls that I picked up cheap in a jumble sale. As the woman down the road said, 'You don't know yer livin'.'

BETH: I'd give you the lot, Theresa, if I could do it without offending anybody. Stephen's house is already coming down with china that belonged to his family.

THERESA: Including a complete set of Belleek, you mother tells me.

BETH: She tells everybody. Some day, I'm going to give her that Belleek tea-set.

THERESA: Don't you like it?

BETH: It's really beautiful, but it symbolises a lot more to my mother than it ever will to me. Do you know, one day we were up at the house and she was gazing at it, and I offered to make a drop of tea and serve it to her in one of the Belleek cups and saucers. She nearly had a fit at the very idea. 'That's for looking at not drinking out of', she said . . . I sometimes think that about Stephen . . .

THERESA: Think what?

BETH: That he's for looking at, for . . . show, not for everyday use . . .

There is a silence. THERESA *looks at* BETH *curiously and then puts her arm around her.*

THERESA: Come on now . . . I think this is called wedding eve jitters . . . you do love him?

BETH: Oh yes . . . at least . . . I think so . . . I'm not sure what love is . . .

THERESA: Ask youself, would you still love him if he was a welder in the shipyard?

BETH: Then he wouldn't be Stephen.

THERESA: You're quite right, that was a daft thing to say . . . go on, admit it, you're marrying him for the Belleek tea-set, aren't you?

BETH: Oh Theresa, I hope not.

THERESA: Beth . . . you don't have to get married . . . do you?

BETH: No, nothing like that . . . Stephen is very . . . respectable.

THERESA: There's still time to change your mind.

BETH: Do you want me to break my mother's heart? She adores him.

THERESA: Do you adore him?

BETH: Oh, this is silly, you're quite right, it's just an attack of wedding eve jitters . . . I've been sitting up here too long on my own. Let's go downstairs and have a drink, eh?

THERESA: Why have you been sitting up here on your own?

BETH: I just sat down for a while, and got to thinking . . . I'm getting married tomorrow, I'm moving from my mother's house to Stephen's house . . . I've been my mother's daughter, and now I'm going to be Stephen's wife . . . I've never been just me. I've never made a decision in my life, Theresa.

THERESA: You decided to get married.

BETH: After Stephen's aunt died, he suddenly said to me one day, 'Let's get married, I'm lonely in that big old house all by myself.' I don't even remember saying yes . . . I wonder what would have happened to me if I'd gone to London with you?

THERESA: Do you want to hear what happened to me?

BETH: I know what happened to you, your mother told me. You have a lovely flat of your own, a fantastic job, independence, and in spite of countless offers, you prefer to be single . . .

THERESA: So that's what she's been saying? Beth, I have two rooms in a depressing house in a seedy London suburb. I have a boring job in the city which I can't leave because I need the money . . . I also have a three-year-old child.

BETH: What?

THERESA: That's why I can't leave the boring job. It pays well, and the hours fit in with Shauna's day nursery.

BETH: Shauna?

THERESA: My daughter . . . This is all top secret, Beth. For God's sake don't tell a soul. I promised my mother I wouldn't disgrace her in front of the neighbours.

BETH: You're not married then.

THERESA: Married! I told him I was pregnant on a Tuesday, by Thursday he was gone. I just heard recently that he got married . . . probably to some nice clever well-brought-up girl who made him wait until she'd got a wedding ring safely on her finger.

BETH: Does he know he has a daughter?

THERESA: Oh, I'm sure he does, there's a flourishing grapevine within the Irish community in London . . . just like home.

BETH: He's Irish?

THERESA: Yes, hilarious, isn't it? I go to London to get away from all this, and I'm hardly off the boat before I fall hook, line and sinker for a sweet-talking, good-looking Catholic boy from Dublin.

BETH: My Great Aunt Maisie always said that them Southern Tagues are the worst.

THERESA: I never thought I'd see the day when I'd be agreeing with your Aunt Maisie.

BETH: How do you manage, alone . . .

THERESA: I cope. It's amazing what you can do if you have to. My mother wanted me to get her adopted, but I wouldn't, and I'm glad. I love her, even if the sight of her scares off prospective husbands. There only seem to be two types of men about, the ones who run away, and the ones who think, 'Wey hey, I'm on to a good thing here' . . . but I live in hope. One day my prince will come.

BETH: So the streets weren't paved with gold after all?

THERESA: They weren't even gilded.

BETH: We're going to London for the honeymoon.

THERESA: For how long?

BETH: About two weeks. Stephen has a couple of business appointments there at the end of the month, we'll be coming back home after that, on the twenty-ninth.

THERESA: That's the day I go back. We'll just miss each other.

SARAH *comes in.*

SARAH: Beth, could you come down for a minute? Mrs McMullan from up the street is here with a present for you and she can only stop for a minute.

BETH: Okay, I'll not be long . . .

BETH *leaves.* SARAH *turns to* THERESA.

SARAH: The neighbours have been awful good. They've bought her some lovely stuff.

THERESA: They have indeed.

SARAH: No sign of you taking the plunge, Theresa?

THERESA: I'm a career girl. Did my mother not tell you?

SARAH *is stroking the head dress and is not really listening.*

SARAH: Just think, this time tomorrow our Beth will be in a private suite in a big London hotel . . . Mrs Stephen Martin. She's done quare and well for herself, hasn't she, Theresa?

THERESA: She's certainly done better than I did.

SARAH *pats* THERESA's *hand comfortingly.*

SARAH: Your time will come, Theresa, you wait and see. A good-lookin' girl like you won't stay single for long.

THERESA: I'm not so sure I want to get married.

SARAH: 'Course you do! You wouldn't want to end up an oul maid, would you? It's not natural for a woman to stay single.

Lights darken on THERESA *and* SARAH *and lighten on* BETH *sitting alone beside a telephone in a hotel bedroom in London. She looks at the shiny new wedding ring on her finger and turns it round. She looks at the phone, then at her watch, then at the phone again. She moves to lift the receiver, changes her mind and opens her handbag. She removes a sprig of white heather. The stem is wrapped in silver foil. She removes some confetti from it, holds the confetti between her fingers and lets it fall to the floor. The phone rings.*

BETH: Hallo? . . . Stephen . . . you said five or ten minutes . . . yes . . . yes . . . I see, no, no I'd rather not come down, I . . . Stephen, I don't really want a drink, . . . and anyway, there's a bottle of champagne here, compliments of the management . . . well, if it's business and it's important, you'd better buy them another drink . . . no I won't . . . I think I'll have a bath . . . it's been a long day . . . yes . . . yes of course I do . . .

She replaces the receiver. She sits very still for a moment, then moves to close her handbag. She stops, looks puzzled, puts her hand in the bag and removes a book. She looks at the title and grins. She phones THERESA.

BETH: Hallo, is that you, Theresa? It's me . . . Beth, I just thought I'd give you a quick ring . . . Stephen? . . . no, he's not here, I mean he's here in the hotel, but he's downstairs at the moment . . . when we arrived there were some business colleagues of Stephen's in the foyer . . . we couldn't get away from them . . . Stephen's buying them a drink to get rid of them . . . no, no, not long, just a few minutes ago . . . Is it really? (*She looks at her watch.*) . . . we were late arriving, the plane was held up . . . (*Desperately.*) Theresa? (*Pause, then calmly.*) . . . I'm ringing to say I've just this minute opened my handbag and found the book . . . very funny! Of course I knew it was you, who else would it be . . . yes, I do remember . . . do you know I've never actually read it? (*She listens and laughs.*) Oh, I am glad I phoned you, I feel better already . . . no, no of course there's nothing wrong . . . listen I'd better go . . . there's a waiter here with champagne . . . Stephen must have ordered it at the bar . . . he'll be here any minute . . . thanks . . . I will. (*She replaces the receiver and looks at the book title.*) The Invisible Man . . . Oh Theresa, if only you knew . . . *She sits, turning the wedding ring round on her finger, quietly, in the distance is heard the sound of BETH and THERESA as children singing 'On the hill there stands a lady, who she is I do not know, all she wants is gold and silver, all she wants is a nice young man.'*

The lights darken. The stage stays dark for a few moments to mark the passing of time. The children's singing merges with radio reports of the 'troubles' in the North. There is the sound of gunfire. The stage lightens to show

SARAH *in the house that once belonged to the* GRANDPARENTS. *Below the three photos of the* GRANDFATHER, SAMUEL *and* SAMMY *is a china cabinet. A large photo of* BETH *and* STEPHEN *on their wedding day is on top of the cabinet. The year is 1971.*

SARAH *is very nervous. She is dusting the china cabinet and keeps looking out of the window at each sound of disturbance. She turns apprehensively as she hears the front door open.* BETH *rushes in.*

SARAH: Beth, what are you doing out in the middle of all this?

BETH: I've been worried sick about you. Your phone's dead, do you know that?

SARAH: I know . . . the electricity's been goin' off and on too . . . you shouldn't have come away over here, there's been shootin' and an explosion . . . is Stephen with you?

BETH: He's abroad on business.

SARAH: You mean you came the whole way here all by yourself? You could have been killed . . . oh, but I am glad to see you . . . you've no idea what it's been like since the internment started . . . bin lids bangin' and riots in the streets . . . and . . .

She begins to cry. BETH *puts her arms around her.*

BETH: You can't stay here alone. You have got to come home with me.

SARAH: I can't leave my house.

BETH: You'll have to . . .

SARAH: I won't . . . it's all I've got . . .

BETH: You've got me . . .

SARAH: I'm not abandoning this house . . .

BETH: Mum, you have no idea how bad it is out there. It's not only shooting and rioting . . . people are leaving their houses, Protestants and Catholics.

Some of the houses at the bottom of this road are ablaze. They're burning the houses as they leave.

SARAH: Who are?

BETH: Both sides. Frightened, desperate people are burning their own houses to stop other frightened desperate people from moving in.

SARAH: And you're askin' me to leave?

BETH: Please, please come home with me.

SARAH *looks at the photos and touches the china cabinet.*

SARAH: No . . . no, this is my home.

There is a loud banging on the door and shouts. The two women look scared. BETH *walks slowly towards the door.*

SARAH: Beth, be careful . . .

BETH *opens the door and returns with a* YOUTH.

YOUTH: We're evacuating the street, missus, you have to get out.

SARAH: And who are you when you're at home?

YOUTH: We're your local defence committee.

SARAH: Well, clear away off and defend us then.

YOUTH: There are too many Catholics in this street. A lot of the Protestants have already been intimidated out. We've orders to move the rest of yous to safety.

SARAH: I moved into this house after my mother and father died. Three generations of my family have lived here, three generations. No IRA gunman is goin' to intimidate me out . . . no, nor no Protestant defence committee neither.

BETH *puts her arms around* SARAH.

BETH: Mum, please let's just go.

SARAH: No.

YOUTH: We've orders to burn these houses.

SARAH *moves defensively in front of the china cabinet.*

SARAH: Over my dead body . . .

BETH: Mum, please . . .

SARAH: You'll not burn my house, nor all the stuff in it. We worked hard all our lives for what's here. It may not be much, but it's mine and nobody's goin' to set fire to it . . .

YOUTH: We have orders . . .

SARAH: From who? To hell with your orders . . . get out of my house . . . get out . . .

She moves as if to attack the YOUTH. *There is the sound of a heavy vehicle outside. The* YOUTH *looks out of the window.*

YOUTH: It's the fuckin' army. They're liftin' everybody in sight. Prods or Fenians, it makes no difference to them bastards.

He exits by the rear door of the house shouting threateningly as he goes.

YOUTH: I'll go out the back way. I'm warnin' you two — get out of here and quick — if we don't come back the IRA will . . . Either way, your house is goin' to burn.

He runs out.

BETH: Mum, I'm not asking you any more, I'm telling you, we have to go . . .

SARAH *looks around the room at the china cabinet and the photos.*

SARAH: I'm not leavin' my wee house, I won't abandon them . . .

BETH: We can bring the pictures with us . . .

SARAH: It's not just the pictures . . .

BETH: Look, I'll put all the china, linen, anything you want into the car . . .

SARAH: My mother worked her fingers to the bone to buy that new devon grate . . .

BETH: The cooker, the kitchen sink,

anything you want . . .

SARAH: I remember the day the men came to put it in. She was that pleased, no more black leadin' . . . that was when she started to buy the brass ornaments, one every nigh and again when she could afford it . . .

BETH: Mum, they're only . . . things . . . bits and pieces . . . they can all be replaced . . .

SARAH: They're my life!!

There is silence for a moment. An ARMY SERGEANT enters.

SERGEANT. A man was seen entering these premises. Does he live here?

BETH glances towards the back door. The SERGEANT moves towards this.

SARAH: You'd be wastin' your time. You wouldn't know the way of the entries.

SERGEANT: Have you been threatened? (*The two women don't reply. He looks with interest at the photos.*) I see you're on our side anyway.

SARAH: Aye, but whose side are you on?

SERGEANT: We're here to keep law and order.

SARAH: Law and order. That's a laugh . . . three generations of my family have fought in your army, and for what? That's my father, gassed in the First World War, that's my brother, killed in the Second, and that's my son, my only son, and he can't even come home on leave any more in case he gets a bullet in his back. The IRA shot an oul lad in the next street the other day, an ex-serviceman. He was goin' to the British Legion for a re-union dinner. Wearin' all his medals, he was, proud as punch. If they'll do the like of that to a harmless old man, what they could do to my Sammy doesn't bear thinkin' about.

SERGEANT: Do the two of you live here alone?

BETH: I'm her married daughter, I live across town.

SERGEANT: Perhaps you should go there. This is a very tense situation tonight. I'm not sure we're going to be able to contain it. And she's probably at special risk with a serving soldier in the family.

BETH: She won't leave.

SERGEANT: Think over what I've said. We haven't enough troops to protect every house.

SARAH: I'm not leavin'.

The SERGEANT moves towards the door followed by BETH.

SERGEANT: Try to persuade her, will you?

BETH: I'll try.

SERGEANT: Where's your brother stationed?

BETH: Cyprus.

SERGEANT: Cyprus. I fought there . . . at least there you could recognise the enemy. Here they all look the same.

BETH: You can tell the Catholics by their close-set eyes. Did nobody ever tell you that?

SERGEANT: No, but I'll bear it in mind. Good night.

BETH: Good night.

The SERGEANT leaves. BETH looks at SARAH who is caressing the china cabinet.

SARAH: I'm not leaving, so you needn't bother trying to persuade me.

BETH: All right, I'll stay here with you then . . . God, I almost wish they would burn this house down, then you'd have to leave, you'd have no choice . . .

SARAH: That's a terrible thing to say, Beth.

BETH (*tiredly*): I'll make a cup of tea.

The lights darken. BETH *steps out of the darkness and addresses the audience.*

BETH: The Army managed to contain the violence, and there were no more houses burned that night. The family house, plus a few others, stood forlornly, defiantly amid the blackened ruins of what the media called 'people's little palaces'. The rattle of the bin-lid had challenged the supremacy of the Lambeg drum. From that night onwards my mother began to die. The doctor's diagnosis was depression. It would pass, he said, it was just her age. It was his standard diagnosis for all his female patients no matter what age they were. The troubles couldn't shift her, but undetected cancer did within the year.

BETH *crosses the stage abruptly and sits down in the empty sofa.*
THERESA *comes in. She has been visiting* SARAH *in the bedroom.*

THERESA: She was talking away, and suddenly she fell asleep in mid-sentence.

BETH: Yes, it happens all the time now, more and more often, it's all the drugs.

THERESA: Well, at least she's not in bad pain (BETH *looks up sharply.*) . . . because of the drugs I mean . . .

BETH: We must all be thankful for small mercies . . . God's good, as my grandmother used to say.

THERESA *stares at her.* BETH *looks away.*

THERESA: You shouldn't be coping with this all on your own, Beth.

BETH: It's amazing what you can do if you have to.

THERESA: Can't Sammy get compassionate leave from the Army?

BETH: Sammy doesn't know how ill she is. She's afraid that if he comes home he might get shot by the IRA. 'There's nothing he can do here,' she said, 'and one dead hero's enough for any family.'

THERESA: You should tell him anyway.

BETH: A bit late in the day, don't you think, for me to start defying my mother?

THERESA: And what about Stephen?

BETH: What about Stephen?

THERESA: When's he coming home from America?

BETH: He's not.

THERESA: Oh . . . I see . . .

BETH (*sarcastically*): Do you?

THERESA (*levelly*): No, I don't actually.

BETH: . . . My father gambled in half-crowns and ten-shilling notes. Stephen gambles in thousands of pounds and bits of paper called stocks and shares. When my father had blown his entire pay packet at the dog track, and was too ashamed to come home, he used to hide out with one of his married sisters. When Stephen's creditors began to hammer on the door, he fled to his aunt in America. She's a wealthy widow and she has no son.

THERESA: Why didn't you ever mention any of this in your letters?

BETH: I come from a long line of respectable women, who never let themselves down in front of the neighbours.

THERESA: I was never one of the neighbours.

BETH: No, you're the one that got away.

THERESA: Why are you angry with me?

BETH: I'm not angry with you . . . I'm just angry.

THERESA: Why?

BETH: Because it's all a lie . . . and I want to tell *her* about it . . . and I can't. My marriage has been the one big success of her life, and I can't

spoil it for her, not now. I can't tell
her that I faithfully repeated all her
mistakes, that if you take away the
velvet sofas and the china cabinets . . .
there's nothing there . . . it's all a
lie . . .

THERESA: So, what are you going to
do about it?

BETH: I can't do anything about it.

THERESA: Why not?

BETH: Because I have to look after her.

THERESA: And what about afterwards?

BETH: Afterwards?

THERESA: After she dies.

BETH: I don't want to talk about this.

THERESA: Will you stay on here?

BETH: I . . . I don't know . . .

THERESA: Will you go back to your
mother's old house?

BETH: It's not her house. Her family
rented it for three generations. I'm
the first one who ever owned a house,
that's another reason for her pride in
me.

THERESA: You could come to London,
stay with me and Shauna for a while.

BETH: I'll think about it.

THERESA: Don't just think about it.
Do something about it.

BETH: Don't you tell me what I should
do! All my life people have been
telling me what I should do!

THERESA: Maybe because all your
life you have let them!

BETH (stiffly): You'd better go. You've
to meet your mother in town. You'll
be late.

THERESA: Shall I come and see you
tomorrow?

BETH: If you like.

There is an awkward silence.

THERESA: Beth . . . I didn't mean
to . . .

BETH (tiredly): It's all right . . . it's
all right . . . you didn't tell me
anything I didn't already know . . .
I'm scared, Theresa . . . my mother's
dying and very soon for the first time
in my life I am going to be alone . . .
and I'm scared . . . my head is full of
other people's memories I don't know
who I am . . . or what I am . . .

THERESA: That's all right. I'm nearly
thirty, and I still don't know what I
want to be when I grow up.

BETH (smiling): Oh, Theresa . . .

THERESA: That's better. I'll come and
see you tomorrow, and I'll tell you
about my grotty flat in London and
my mad teenage daughter. Then you'll
definitely not want to come.

*They exit. SARAH enters, slowly,
painfully. She lies down on the velvet
sofa. BETH returns.*

SARAH: Has Theresa gone?

BETH: She had to meet her mother in
town. She'll be back to see us
tomorrow . . . why won't you stay in
bed?

SARAH: Because I love being in this
room . . . all the same, Beth, you have
to admit I'm going out in quare
style . . . velvet sofas and fine bone
china and the Orangemen paradin'
past the window . . .

BETH's *face contorts as if she doesn't
know whether to laugh or cry.*

BETH: Would you like a cup of tea?

SARAH: In a minute.

*She takes two wedding rings off her
finger and holds them out to BETH.*

SARAH: Here, I want you to wear these.

BETH: Why?

SARAH: They'll guard you after I'm
gone, my wedding ring and your
granny's. They'll keep you safe, put
them on, child.

BETH: Why now?

SARAH: Because I know you. If I die with them on you'll never wear them . . . and I want you to wear them, for luck. Wedding rings are charms, you know.

She puts the rings on BETH's *right hand.*

SARAH: Now I'll have that cup of tea you were offerin'.

BETH: Do you know what I'm going to do?

SARAH: What?

BETH: I'm going to get one of those Belleek cups and saucers out of that cabinet in the dining room and serve you tea in it.

SARAH: You can't do that.

BETH: I can if I want . . .

SARAH: I suppose you can, it belongs to you . . .

BETH: That's right . . . wouldn't you like to be the very first person to have actually had a drink out of that set?

SARAH: Don't tempt me.

BETH: That's exactly what I'm going to do, I won't be a minute.

She goes to get the Belleek. SARAH *sits back, smiling in anticipation. Her dead brother,* SAMUEL, *appears in Second World War Uniform.*

SARAH: Oh, Samuel, I thought you were never coming.

BETH *returns with the Belleek cup and saucer in her hand. She thinks that* SARAH *is asleep again, but slowly realises that she is dead. She sets the cup and saucer down and strokes* SARAH's *hair. The stage darkens.* BETH *walks out of the darkness and addresses the audience.*

BETH: I had a long time to prepare myself for her death. I used to sit and watch her sleeping and find myself wondering what I would do first, when it happened. Would I phone Sammy, send for a minister, a doctor, an undertaker? I did all of those things later, but first of all I covered the mirrors in the house with white starched linen cloths, just as my grandmother had shown me, so that the evil spirits could not reflect away her soul.

The whole stage lightens on the family house and BETH's *house. (* SARAH *is no longer on the velvet sofa).* BETH *walks to the three photos of the family soldiers and takes them off the wall. She carried them to the velvet sofa and sets them in a row. A woman (a* VALUER *from an auction house) comes in with a list of the contents of* BETH's *house on a clipboard.*

VALUER: I've put an approximate valuation on everything in the house. 'Course, with auctions, you never know, you might get more, you might get less. Do you want a reserve price on anything?

BETH: No, just sell the lot for whatever you can get.

VALUER: Whatever you say.

BETH: You'll be here when they come to pack it all up?

VALUER: Oh, I'll be here. You have some valuable pieces. We don't want any of it broken.

BETH: You'll need the house keys.

She hands her the keys.

VALUER: What'll I do with the keys after?

BETH: Pass them on to the solicitor, with the money.

VALUER: I'm sure you'll be sorry to leave this lovely house.

BETH: I won't be sorry at all.

VALUER: If I'd the money I'd buy it myself.

BETH: Is your list complete now?

VALUER: It is . . . a pity about the Belleek tea-set.

BETH: What?

VALUER: The Belleek tea-set, there's a cup and saucer missing. Didn't you know?

BETH: Oh yes . . . I did . . . they got broken, a long time ago.

VALUER: Pity about that. It's still worth a bit of money of course, but if the set had been complete, it would have fetched maybe three or four times as much.

She peers at the Army photos on the velvet sofa.

BETH: They were my mother's. They're not part of this house.

VALUER: They're not worth anything anyway. Old wartime photos, cheap frames . . . there's a lot of them about.

BETH: Yes, I'm sure there are.

VALUER: Well, I'd better be off. It was a real pleasure valuing your stuff, Mrs Martin, a real pleasure. Lovely, some of it, lovely . . . pity about the Belleek tea set though.

She leaves. BETH smiles after her. She opens her handbag and takes out a small tissue-wrapped parcel. She removes the tissue paper, looks at the Belleek cup and saucer, and smiles. She sings quietly to herself 'On the hill there stands a lady, who she is I do not know . . . ' As she sings she wraps up the Belleek cup and saucer and carefully replaces it in her hand bag. She walks off the stage, still singing.

JOYRIDERS

Joyriders takes place mainly in the former Lagan Linen Mill where the Youth Training Programme now operates. There is one scene in a Belfast theatre, one in Kate's house, one in the Arts Council Gallery, Belfast.

The walls of the linen mill are decorated with the teenagers' paintings of Belfast street life and samples of the work produced on the knitting machines. There is a lot of graffiti, mainly in the form of abbreviations:

F.T.P.	FUCK THE POPE
F.T.Q.	FUCK THE QUEEN
U.T.H.	UP THE HOODS
I.R.A.	IRISH REPUBLICAN ARMY
I.N.L.A.	IRISH NATIONAL LIBERATION FRONT
U.D.A.	ULSTER DEFENCE ASSOCIATION
U.V.F.	ULSTER VOLUNTEER FORCE
L.P.W.	LOYALIST PRISONERS OF WAR
L.F.C.	LINFIELD FOOTBALL CLUB
C.F.C.	CELTIC FOOTBALL CLUB
G.F.C.	GLENTORAN FOOTBALL CLUB

There are also some slogans:

No Pope Here – No friggin' wonder
Fuck 1690. We want a re-run
The Pope is a Para – Paisley for Pope
God save Ulster/The Queen/The Pope/Us
God Love Big Sandra
Jesus saves with the Abbey National
Give us a job. What's a job?
Is there a life before death?
Snuff is high class glue.
Joyriders live. Joyriders die.

The mixture of Protestant/Catholic graffiti is due mainly to jokers, but also because there will be a small number of Protestant teenagers among the predominantly Catholic teenagers on the course.

This particular training programme is mainly peopled by young offenders on probation or suspended sentence for petty crime and joyriding.

Cast

SANDRA   Aged 16–17. Tough, cynical, intelligent. Protects herself by refusing to believe in or aspire to anything.

MAUREEN   Aged 16–17. Hopeful, dreamy, Lives alone with and constantly worried about her 12-year-old brother Johnnie who is a compulsive joyrider and glue-sniffer.

ARTHUR   Aged 17–18. A skinhead by accident rather than choice. Was accidentally shot by the army. His injuries have left him with a shaven head, a scarred face and a limp. He looks dangerous/menacing, but is in general a cheerful joker.

TOMMY   Aged 17–18. Slight physical signs of possible mixed racial parentage. Interested in politics. Steals for himself and for others.

KATE   Aged 34. A social worker in charge of the Youth Training Programme that the four teenagers are attending. Middle class, concerned, committed. Frustrated by the futility of the scheme. Tries to interest the teenagers in theatre, art, and so on.

Joyriders was commissioned and produced by Paines Plough, The Writers Company, and opened at the Tricycle Theatre on 13 February 1986, prior to a nationwide tour with the following cast.

SANDRA	Michelle Fairley
MAUREEN	Clare Cathcart
ARTHUR	Gerard O'Hare
TOMMY	Fabian Cartwright
KATE	Veronica Duffy

Voice-overs in *Shadow of a Gunman*

MRS GRIGSON	Sheila Hancock
DONAL DAVOREN	Stephen Rea
SEAMUS SHIELDS	John Thaw

Director	Pip Broughton
Designer	Ellen Cairns
Lighting Designer	Jim Simmons
Assistant Director	Jeremy Raison
Stage Managers	Margaret Sutherland
	Robin Nash
	Imogen Bertin

The songs in *Joyriders* were written and first performed by residents of Divis Flats working with Clair Chapman. For information on where to obtain musical scores etc., apply to Goodwin Associates 12 Rabbit Row, Kensington Church Street, London W8 4DX.

In November 1985, the Divis Residents Association and the Town and Country Planning Association, London, held an exhibition of photographs of the Divis Flats complex in Belfast, which was described as the worst housing development in Western Europe. These flats provide the background for *Joyriders*.

The action of the play takes place between February and May 1986.

PROLOGUE

Belfast Street Song

FIRST VOICE:	Everywhere we go
SECOND VOICE:	Everywhere we go
FIRST VOICE:	People always ask us
SECOND VOICE:	People always ask us
FIRST VOICE:	Who we are
SECOND VOICE:	Who we are
FIRST VOICE:	And where do we come from
SECOND VOICE:	And where do we come from
FIRST VOICE:	And we always tell them
SECOND VOICE:	And we always tell them
FIRST VOICE:	We're from Belfast
SECOND VOICE:	We're from Belfast
FIRST VOICE:	Mighty mighty mighty mighty mighty mighty Belfast
SECOND VOICE:	Mighty mighty mighty mighty mighty mighty Belfast
FIRST VOICE:	And if they can't hear us
SECOND VOICE:	And if they can't hear us
FIRST VOICE:	We shout a little louder
SECOND VOICE:	We shout a little louder

(Repeat song louder, and an octave higher. End with:
'And if they can't hear us, they must be deaf')

ACT ONE

Mid-February 1986.

A theatre in Belfast. KATE, SANDRA,
MAUREEN, ARTHUR *and* TOMMY
*watching the end of Sean O'Casey's play
'Shadow of a Gunman'.* KATE *and*
TOMMY *both watch intently.* ARTHUR
is grinning. SANDRA *is bored.*
MAUREEN *is in tears. Sound of explosion,
gunfire, then voice over.*

Scene One

VOICE OVER (*Mrs Grigson*): What's
goin' to happen next? Oh, Mr Davoren,
isn't it terrible? Isn't it terrible?
Minnie Powell, poor little Minnie
Powell's been shot dead! They were
raidin' a house a few doors down, an'
had just got up in their lorries to go
away, when they was ambushed. You
never heard such shootin'. An' in the
thick of it, poor Minnie went to jump
off the lorry she was on, an' she was
shot through the bozzum. (ARTHUR
grins at the word bozzom, nudges
SANDRA). Oh it was horrible to see
the blood pourin' out, an' Minnie
moanin'. They found some paper in
her breast (ARTHUR *nudges*
SANDRA *again*) with Minnie written
on it, an' some other name they
couldn't make out with the blood;
the officer kep' it. The ambulance is
bringin' her to the hospital, but what
good's that when she's dead. Poor
little Minnie, poor little Minnie Powell,
to think of you full of a life a few
minutes ago, an' now she's dead!

VOICE OVER (*Donal Davoren*): Ah me,
alas! Pain, pain, pain ever for ever. It's
terrible to think that poor little
Minnie is dead, but it's still more
terrible to think that Davoren and
Shields are alive! Oh, Donal Davoren,
shame is your portion now till the
silver cord is loosened and the golden
bowl be broken. Oh Davoren, Donal
Davoren, poet and poltroon, poltroon
and poet!

VOICE OVER (*Seumas Shields*): I knew
something ud come of the tappin' on
the wall.

Sounds of audience applause. KATE
and MAUREEN *applaud.* TOMMY
and SANDRA *do not applaud.*
ARTHUR *gives a slow handclap,
whistles.*

ARTHUR *and* SANDRA *go to get up.*

KATE: We might as well sit here until
the crowd clears.

TOMMY: What for? Are we not good
enough to mingle with the fur-coat
brigade in the foyer?

ARTHUR: You know what they say
Sandra? Fur coat, no knickers.

SANDRA *takes out a cigarette.*

KATE: Sandra, I've already told you, no
smoking in the auditorium.

ARTHUR: Are you allowed to piss in the
auditorium? Only, I need to go now.

KATE: Arthur, you went four times
during the play. You couldn't need to
go again.

ARTHUR: I've got a damaged bladder.

KATE: No you haven't. You were
injured in the head and legs. All the
parts in between are in perfect
working order.

ARTHUR (*leering at* SANDRA): That's
true.

SANDRA: Piss off Arthur.

ARTHUR: Are you all right Maureen?

MAUREEN: You're rotten. Laughin'
when the girl got shot.

ARTHUR: How could ye feel sorry for
a girl called Minnie?

SANDRA: She was pathetic. Gettin'
killed to save him.

MAUREEN: She was brave. It was lovely.

TOMMY: It wasn't lovely. (*He speaks
slowly as if quoting from a political
text book.*) It was a comment on what
happens to people what are kep' down

by the yoke of British imperialism.

ARTHUR: Is that what it was? I thought he just wanted to screw her, but he hadn't the nerve.

SANDRA: All talk, like you Arthur.

ARTHUR: Come roun' the back an' talk to me then.

MAUREEN: Minnie loved him, that's why she died for him.

SANDRA: He wouldn't die for her though, would he? Some hero. All mouth, no action.

KATE: That's why O'Casey called him the Shadow of a Gunman.

ARTHUR: He was a five-star wanker.

MAUREEN: He was a poet.

SANDRA: He was a shite.

TOMMY: He was a nuthin'. People like him what sit on the political fence live on while the innocent die.

SANDRA: Tommy, you must be the most borin' person on God's earth.

ARTHUR: He's the one what's all talk, like him in the play . . . whadye-callhim . . .

KATE: Davoren, Donal Davoren.

TOMMY: Whadye mean?

ARTHUR: All his big ideas come from books. So do yours.

TOMMY: I don't just read about it. I know a few of the lads.

SANDRA: We all know a few of the lads. They live in the same rotten housin' on the same rotten road we do.

TOMMY: I've done them a few small favours.

ARTHUR: Like what?

TOMMY: Nothin' I can talk about.

ARTHUR: Because you've got nuthin' to talk about, that's why. Yer all mouth.

MAUREEN: Donal really loved Minnie.

SANDRA: Aye, enough to let her die.

You're as soft as she was. Kate, can we go now, I'm dying' fer a feg.

ARTHUR: An' my willie's bustin'.

SANDRA: Arthur, do you never think of nuthin' else? You think you're God's gift.

ARTHUR: When I get my compensation fer the accident, you'll all be after my body.

SANDRA: Arthur, I wouldn't have ye if ye were studded with diamonds.

ARTHUR: You'd have me, wouldn't ye Maureen?

SANDRA: Maureen's in love with Nik Kershaw.

MAUREEN: I like his records.

SANDRA (sings mockingly): Wouldn't it be good to be in your shoes, even if it was for just one day . . .

TOMMY, SANDRA, ARTHUR (sing): Wouldn't it be good if we could wish our cares away . . .

KATE: Well, as the philosophical discussion on the play appears to be over, I'll go and get the car. You wait here. It's still raining. No point in us all getting soaked. I'll see you in the foyer in about five minutes.

ARTHUR: You givin' us all a lift home, Kate?

KATE: Right to your front doors. That way you'll get to bed early and be in on time in the morning.

SANDRA: Any word of me gettin' off them stupid knittin' machines and onto car maintenance?

KATE: I've already had a word with the project leader. I've to see him again at the end of the week.

SANDRA: He doesn't want me there, does he?

KATE: He thinks you wouldn't be strong enough to handle a lot of the work.

SANDRA: I'm bigger than half them wee lads doin' it.

ARTHUR: Weemin don't repair cars.

SANDRA: If you can do caterin' I can change a sparkin' plug.

ARTHUR: All the greatest chefs is men.

SANDRA: Aye, because women get landed with the cookin' jobs that pay buttons, or nuthin' at all.

KATE: I'll get the car.

She exits.

MAUREEN: It must be lovely to have yer own car. Drive out till the country an' all.

SANDRA: Get your Johnnie to steal one for ye.

MAUREEN: Johnnie doesn't do that no more.

SANDRA: You mean he hasn't got caught for a while.

MAUREEN: He's stopped. He's working hard at school.

SANDRA: Tell that to the probation officer.

ARTHUR: Maybe I'll buy a car out of my compensation.

TOMMY: You haven't a hope in hell of gettin' compensation.

ARTHUR: My solicitor says we have a good case.

TOMMY: The British Army have the best case goin'. The courts is on their side. No judge here is gonna convict a soldier of attempted murder.

ARTHUR: It's not that sort of case. Nobody's on trial. Nobody has to get convicted of nuthin'. All my solicitor has to prove is that the Brits opened fire on a joyrider an' I got hit by accident. He has to prove that I wasn't doin't nuthin'.

TOMMY: Maureen's ma wasn't doin' nuthin'. She didn't get no compensation.

There was a silence at the mention of MAUREEN's *mother.*

SANDRA: Shut up Tommy. Come on Maureen and we'll have a smoke.

MAUREEN: I haven't got no fegs.

SANDRA: We'll share one.

The girls exit.

ARTHUR: We'll all go to the bar, share a pint before Kate gets back.

TOMMY: They won't serve us.

ARTHUR: They won't know we're under age.

TOMMY: I don't mean that. Did ye see the way they looked at us when we come in? This is a middle-class theatre. Not for the likes of us.

ARTHUR: My money's as good as anybody else's.

TOMMY: How much have ye got left out of Maggie Thatcher's twenty-seven poun' thirty pence?

ARTHUR: Enough to buy a pint.

TOMMY: I bet ye a poun' they won't serve ye.

ARTHUR: Yer on. Here, if they don't serve us, how'll we know why?

TOMMY: By the way they look at ye.

SONG: 'Children of Divis Flats'

We are the children of Divis Flats
And it's for houses that we're
fighting   Repeat

A place to live a place to play
A place for health and happiness
                                      Repeat

They took our houses they gave us flats
How much longer must we live here?
                                      Repeat

We are the children of Divis Flats
And it's for houses that we're fighting
                                      Repeat

Among the rats, among the clocks[1]
And breathing in asbestos   Repeat

[1] 'Clocks' are Belfast cockroaches.

We are the children of Divis Flats
And it's for houses that we're fighting
Repeat

Scene Two

The Lagan Mill. The following morning.
TOMMY *comes in, looks around to make sure no one is about. Lifts a catering bag of tea bags, tosses it to someone offstage. Lifts a catering tin of coffee, tosses it to someone offstage. Goes to a clock card machine. Clocks in. Exits.* MAUREEN *enters, clocks in, goes and sits down at a knitting machine. Looks at her watch, goes to* KATE's *phone, dials.*

MAUREEN: Hello, is that you, Mr McAuley. It's Maureen Reilly. Our Johnnie's not well, he won't be into school the day . . . what? . . . he's got . . . a cold . . . and a sore throat . . . he'll be in the morra . . . no he's not mitchin', he's not well, so he's not.

KATE *comes in, overhears part of the conversation.*

MAUREEN: Sorry Kate, I would've asked, but ye weren't about.

KATE: It's all right.

MAUREEN: I'll see ye later.

KATE: Maureen?

MAUREEN: What?

KATE: Sit down a minute.

MAUREEN: I've a lot on the day.

KATE: What's the matter with Johnnie?

MAUREEN: He's not well.

KATE: What way not well? (*Pause.*) Has he been on the glue again?

MAUREEN: No . . . I don't know . . . he was in bed when I got home last night. About six o'clock this mornin' I heard him vomitin'. He was as sick as a dog.

KATE: Where is he now?

MAUREEN: In the house. He's all right, just a bit green aroun' the gills. He'll sleep it off. He got fish an' chips in Larry's last night. I'm always tellin' him not to eat anything out of that dirty hole. The health man shoulda closed that dive down years ago. I don't know how that oul Larry gets away with it.

KATE: When does Johnnie see his probation officer again?

MAUREEN: Friday.

KATE: I think you should give her a call today.

MAUREEN: No.

KATE: Maureen, Claudia's job is to help Johnnie and you. She's on your side.

MAUREEN: She works for them, and they wanta put Johnnie away.

KATE: Her job is to prevent that happening.

MAUREEN: You shoulda seen the oul magistrate, old as the hills kep' sayin' to me 'Speak up, girl, I can't hear you.' As if it was my fault he was half deaf. He told our Johnnie if he got caught doin' anything again he'd put him away an' no more chances.

KATE: He would have been put in a home if Claudia hadn't convinced the magistrate that you were capable and reliable and fit to look after him. She made promises on your behalf, Maureen. Don't let her down. You have got to let her know if Johnnie's on the glue again.

MAUREEN: He's not. It was Larry's oul re-heated fish.

KATE: If he's sniffing again, he'll be out joyriding before the week's out.

MAUREEN: I told you. He's not sniffin' nuthin'. That Larry has a lot to answer for.

KATE: Claudia will have a lot to answer for if Johnnie gets himself injured, or injures somebody else.

MAUREEN: You're not worried about our Johnnie nor me. You're just afraid yer chum Claudia'll get intil trouble for not doin' her job right.

KATE: I'm afraid that Johnnie might get shot.

MAUREEN: Don't say that.

KATE: Not saying it doesn't mean it's not happening.

MAUREEN: The ones what got shot were big lads. Our Johnnie's only twelve.

TOMMY *has come in and overheard part of the conversation.*

TOMMY: I never heard of the security forces checkin' anybody's age, name and address before they opened fire.

MAUREEN *walks out. She passes* ARTHUR *who is clocking in.*

ARTHUR: Mornin' sweetheart.

MAUREEN: Away an' jump.

ARTHUR: What did I say?

He puts on a white coat and a chef's hat. Gets things ready for the morning tea break. Sets out cups, fills the tea urn with water, etc.

KATE: Okay, Tommy. Where's the paint?

TOMMY: What paint?

KATE: Two litres of white gloss, two litres of varnish, and a plastic container of white spirit.

TOMMY: I'm only in. Ask themens in the joinery section.

KATE: I was here very early, long before any of you got in. Stocktaking. The stuff was already gone.

TOMMY: Some bugger broke in durin' the night?

KATE: Stop acting the innocent. It went missing yesterday when you were in charge of the sixteen-year-olds who were painting the lockers.

TOMMY: The wee buggers. Wait'll I get the houl of them.

KATE: Has it already been sold?

TOMMY: How would I know?

KATE: Is this one for yourself or are you doing another wee homer? Redecorating some poor old pensioner's flat?

TOMMY: It would take more than a licka paint to make any of them flats fit to live in.

KATE: I want it back, Tommy, and I want it back today.

TOMMY: What's a couple of friggin' tins of paint til the government?

KATE: When you nick paint from here, you're not stealing from the government, you're stealing from your own people.

TOMMY: You can't steal from people who own nuthin'.

KATE: Yes you can Tommy. You can steal away the only chance they have.

TOMMY: Of what! Of workin' fer slave wages? . . . Why are we not allowed to make a profit on what we do here?

KATE: We must not come into competition with local industry.

TOMMY: What local industry! What you mean is, it would be really embarrassing if this underfunded project made a profit. People might start askin' if we can do it, why couldn't John de Lorean.

KATE: Tommy, this project is not about profit . . .

TOMMY: No, it's about keepin' the unemployment figures down and keepin' the likes of us off the streets.

KATE: It also keeps you out of borstal.

TOMMY: An' that's the only reason I'm here. Me an' all the other ones on probation or suspended sentence. Like they said, ye can go on the scheme or get locked up.

KATE: So why don't you help to make it work?

TOMMY: I never promised to enjoy it.

KATE: Tommy, there are a lot of people who would be delighted if this place closed, who never wanted it opened in the first place. They think teenagers like you should be horsewhipped and dropped into a bottomless pit, not trained to do something with all that energy . . .

TOMMY: Trained! Fer what! At the end of the fuckin' year, we'll be back on the fuckin' street with no fuckin' jobs.

KATE: If I fiddle the books anymore, I'll have no job either. I have a year to prove that we can employ young offenders here for a tenth of what it costs to lock them away in approved institutions. If, at the end of the year, we are running at a loss and it can be proved that any of that loss was due to thieving, we've had it. The opposition will rub their sweaty hands with glee and say 'We told you so' and this place will close. (*Pause*.) Do you want to be responsible for proving that all their prejudices are right? (*Pause*.) I want that paint back, Tommy.

TOMMY: I'll have a word. See what I can do . . .

KATE: You want to do something. Try putting your Robin Hood ideas to good use in here. Stop fighting me . . . please . . . I need all the help I can get. (*Pause*.)

TOMMY: I won't hinder ye . . . but I won't help ye neither.

KATE: Well, will you at least help the younger kids who do want to be here?

TOMMY: Nobody wants to be here.

KATE: That's not true. Not everyone on this project came through the courts. Tweny per cent chose to come.

TOMMY: Only because they get eight quid more here than they would on the dole.

KATE: It's not just that. There's a real enthusiasm among a lot of them, even the ones who did come through the courts. They want to make a go of it. They want it to work. For the first time in their lives they have teachers who are genuinely interested in them

and what happens to them . . .

TOMMY: For what we are about to receive may the government make us truly thankful.

KATE: I don't want your gratitude. I want you to stop wrecking this scheme until there's something better to take its place.

ARTHUR *comes in*.

ARTHUR: Hey Kate, there's no tea nor coffee in the kitchen.

TOMMY: Not now Arthur.

KATE: There had better be tea, coffee, sugar and a lot more besides in that kitchen or none of you are going to eat or drink all week. I am not buying as much as an extra pint of milk! Is that clear!

She walks out.

ARTHUR: What did I say? What's the matter with everybody the day? I thought it was goin' to be a good day, you know? I woke up this mornin' and the oul leg wasn't as bad as it sometimes is. I was able til get outa bed myself without havin' to get my ma to do her big Goliath crane act. I think the oul leg's gettin' better. My da says if I stop limpin' before the court case, he'll friggin' kill me.

TOMMY: The tea an' coffee's in one of the lockers in the joinery section. Ask wee Oliver, he'll show you where it is.

ARTHUR: Listen you, you wanna thieve, you do it in your own section. I take a pride in my kitchen so I do.

TOMMY: What's on the menu the day?

ARTHUR: Ragout. (*He pronounces the 'T'*.)

TOMMY: What?

ARTHUR: French for stew.

TOMMY: For Jesus sake, Arthur, nobody here wants anything that doesn't have chips with it.

ARTHUR: I'm doin' chips as well. And

pommes-de-terres. (*He pronounces both 'S's'.*)

TOMMY: What time's yer break?

ARTHUR: Two to three. Why?

TOMMY: What are you doin' then?

ARTHUR: Eatin' the leftovers.

TOMMY: What else are ye doin'?

ARTHUR: Chattin' up big Sandra.

TOMMY: Will you give me a hand to do somethin'?

ARTHUR: What?

TOMMY: I need some money quick. Is that oul deaf guy still operatin' the petrol pump at the garage?

ARTHUR: Ferget it. My case is comin' up. I'm not blowin' that fer a couple of quid out of a cash register.

TOMMY: What'll ye do if ye get the money?

ARTHUR: Make big Sandra an offer she can't refuse.

TOMMY: Don't you have no ambitions?

ARTHUR: Aye, to die of old age.

TOMMY: I mean like helpin' other people.

ARTHUR: What for? Nobody ever helped me.

TOMMY: Come on, I'll get ye the tea an' coffee.

As they exit they bump into SANDRA *as she rushes in.*

ARTHUR: Mornin' darlin'.

SANDRA: Piss off.

ARTHUR (*to* TOMMY): It must be the time of the month or somethin'.

TOMMY *and* ARTHUR *exit.* SANDRA *punches her card. Looks at it.*

SANDRA: Shite!

She goes to MAUREEN *in the knitting machine section.*

SANDRA: One minute past. That's

another fifteen-p off my wages.

MAUREEN: It's ten past.

SANDRA: I'll hafta nick a new watch, this one's hopeless. What's up with you?

MAUREEN: Nuthin'.

SANDRA: You still mopin' about that stupid play?

MAUREEN: It wasn't stupid.

SANDRA: What does it matter why people get shot? If you get shot you get shot and that's all there is to it. (MAUREEN *looks away*.) Is your ma worse, is that what's the matter?

MAUREEN: It's our Johnny. I think he's on the glue again.

SANDRA: He was never off it.

MAUREEN: He was.

SANDRA: He's a no-hoper. He always has been.

MAUREEN: I won't let them take him away.

SANDRA: You'd be better off without him.

MAUREEN: He's all I've got.

SANDRA: He's your brother. The way you talk you'd think he was your son.

MAUREEN: He's nobody's son. My da's God knows where, and my mother . . . She might as well be dead for all she knows.

SANDRA: Are ye goin' up to see her the night?

MAUREEN: I might.

SANDRA: I'll come with ye if ye like.

MAUREEN: What for?

SANDRA: I've nuthin' better to do.

MAUREEN: There's not much to do there. She just sits, starin', sayin' nuthin'.

SANDRA: Does she never speak?

MAUREEN: Every nigh an' again she

opens her mouth as if she's gonna say somethin' an' then she screams. It's awful. They give her an injection an' she sleeps an' when she wakes up she just stares again.

SANDRA: Fuckin' Brits.

MAUREEN: It's not as if she got hurt bad, not like some of them . . . Have you ever seen a plastic bullet?

SANDRA: Loads of them. Every time there's a riot our kid collects them. He's small and he's fast. Dives in an' out between the legs of the Brits and the rioters. He's fuckin' magic to watch.

MAUREEN: What for?

SANDRA: He sells them.

MAUREEN: Who to?

SANDRA: Tourists. Americans mostly, and some of them people what come here and write about us. A pound a bullet he gets. It's better than a paper round. He'll go far our kid. He'll have his own business when the rest of us is still on the dole.

MAUREEN: It's better here than bein' on the dole.

SANDRA: What's better about it, except that you get more money?

MAUREEN: You've got somewhere to go. Somethin' to do.

SANDRA: Like knittin' stupid sweaters that nobody wants.

MAUREEN: I have orders for five more.

SANDRA: Only because they're dirt cheap. I told Kate we'd get more down the market for them than selling them roun' here.

MAUREEN: We're not allowed. Kate has to keep to the rules. If she doesn't, they'll close the place down.

SANDRA: I don't know why they opened it in the first place. It's a friggin' waste of time.

MAUREEN: It's better than hangin'

roun' the house all day.

SANDRA: My granny worked in here. It used to be a linen mill ye know.

MAUREEN: I know. My granny worked here too.

SANDRA: Did she ever tell ye about what it was like?

MAUREEN: She died young. I don't remember.

SANDRA: My granny was one of the lucky ones. Lived long enough to draw the pension. Most of her mates coughed their lungs up or died of lead poisonin' before they were forty. An' they got paid even less than we do.

MAUREEN: It's not that bad nowadays.

SANDRA: No, now ye get to die of cancer or boredom, if the army or the police don't get ye first.

She takes a screwdriver out of her pocket, unscrews part of the knitting machine.

MAUREEN: What are ye doin'?

SANDRA: I'm not doin' this no more. If the machine's broke they'll hafta put me on the cars. Friggin' Lady Summerville.

MAUREEN: Who?

SANDRA: Lady Summerville. She donated the machines. Were you not here the day she come on the visit? The week before Christmas it was.

MAUREEN: I had the flu.

SANDRA: She brought us a turkey. Arthur stuffed it with chestnuts. Friggin' chestnuts! It was diabolical. Anyway, the Lady Summerville give us a wee pep talk about how wonderful we all were, and how she give us the machines because when she was young there was a sewing room in her big house an' the girls from the village come in and made garments for the poor. Life's a geg isn' it?

MAUREEN: Maybe if we asked her, she'd give us a machine when our year's up here. We could go into business on our own.

SANDRA: Maureen, grow up. Nobody is never gonna give us nuthin'.

SONG

What will it be when we leave school
Will it be ace schemes or Y.T.P.
Will it be useful, will it be paid
We'll have to wait and see.

Hope it's work, real work
We hope it's work, real work
We hope it's work, real work
And not the dole.

Scene Three

KATE *sorting out papers on her desk. She lifts a small dictaphone, speaks into it.*

KATE: Molly, I have a meeting this morning with the fund-raising committee, so will you go ahead and type out these progress reports and I'll sign them when I get back. Also, will you type a reply to this letter from Councillor Margaret Anderson. As you will see, she is requesting, among other things, a breakdown on the Catholic/ Protestant ratio of teenagers in each of the sections here. Now what is that bigoted old bat up to now I wonder . . . Give her all the necessary detail . . . we started out with sixty participants and are now down to fifty . . . three have been arrested and the other seven, all Protestants, have been transferred to other schemes at their own request. Make sure she understands there was no intimidation here . . . maybe that's what she's angling for . . . they all left because they were understandably nervous about working in this area . . . oh, and do point out (politely of course) that I did warn the powers that be, this would be a problem when we were offered these premises, not a stone's throw away from I.R.A. territory . . . However, there are still six cheeky, cheerful,

undaunted Protestants in the car maintenance section, and I'm confident they'll stay and complete the course, because they're very keen to participate in the stock-car races we're planning to organise in the summer . . . God and the fund-raising committee willing . . . maybe her husband would like to sponsor us . . . maybe he'd like to offer all the kids here jobs in his factory . . . Tell our beloved councillor there are fifty kids here and we'll be lucky if we can find jobs for five of them at the end of the year, regardless of what religion they are . . . they fuckin' know it, we fuckin' know it, and she fuckin' knows it . . .

She stops as ARTHUR *comes in with a cup of tea, is embarrassed that he has heard her swearing.*

ARTHUR (*grinning*): Cuppa tea, Kate?

KATE: Tea turned up, did it?

ARTHUR: And the coffee. Some dope-head shifted it til another cupboard . . . by mistake.

KATE: Arthur?

ARTHUR: What?

KATE: The old woman who lives next door with all those stray cats. When you give her a free dinner, make sure you get the plates back. We're running low.

ARTHUR: You don't miss much do ye Kate.

KATE: I assume it's leftovers, that you're not making her special meals or giving her free cartons of milk. We can't afford that.

ARTHUR: Here's yer tea.

KATE: Thanks . . . Arthur, if you get this compensation money, will you leave here?

ARTHUR: I'll be eighteen soon. I'll hafta leave then anyway.

KATE: No, you can stay on until the end of the year. (*Pause.*) You're a good cook, a natural.

ARTHUR: It's dead easy. You know them big restaurants must make a fortune. It's as cheap, cheaper, even to make that sort of food fresh than buy it freezed or in a tin, but they get away with chargin' double for it.

KATE: If I could arrange it, would you be interested in coming back next year to teach the new intake about cooking, catering, all that?

ARTHUR: I don't have no exams nor nuthin.'

KATE: Would you be interested?

ARTHUR: I dunno. Would I get paid?

KATE: Yes. Not a lot, but more than twenty-seven pounds and thirty pence.

ARTHUR: Money fer oul jam. They'd never wear it.

KATE: They might.

ARTHUR: Why do ye bother, Kate?

KATE: Because I'm an incurable optimist. I still have a romantic belief that if an idea is good and right, then it's possible. You're a bit of an optimist yourself, Arthur.

ARTHUR: I'm not awful sure what an optimist is . . .

KATE: It's someone who believes that . . . things will turn out all right in the end . . . or at least that it's possible to make things turn out all right.

ARTHUR: Like, if ye wanta be a cook, ye can be a cook?

KATE: Yes.

ARTHUR: They make fun of me round here, ye know. Men don't cook in West Belfast. I don't care. What's so great about bein' a casual labourer on a buildin' site? Ye get soaked to the skin an' wore out before yer time. But you see kitchens? They're magic. Bein' the youngest, I was always home from school first. Mondays in the winter was the best. My ma always did two things on a Monday, she did the weekend washin' an' she made a big pot of vegetable broth. The kitchen walls would be streamin' with the steam from the washin' and the soup, an' I'd come in freezin' an' my ma would light the gas oven an' I'd take off the wet shoes an' socks an' put my feet in the oven an' sit drinkin' a cup of the soup . . . soapsuds an' vegetables . . . it sounds revoltin' but it was great . . .

(He becomes self conscious about what he is saying.)

You don't know what I'm bletherin' on about, do ye?

KATE: Smells.

ARTHUR: What?

KATE: Smells . . . my mother smells of lavender water and silk. Expensive but discreet, and in terribly good taste . . . Did your mother really let you warm your feet in the oven?

ARTHUR: We don't have no central heatin'.

KATE: (*laughing wryly at herself*): I will get you a job here, Arthur, if only to stop me getting romantic notions about things which are purely practical . . . and now you don't know what I'm blethering on about, do you?

ARTHUR: I know yer sorta puttin' yerself down. Yer always doin' that. You shouldn't. Yer too good fer in here.

KATE: What's a nice girl like me doing in a place like this?

ARTHUR: What?

KATE: It's a saying . . . from the Hollywood movies . . . you've never heard it.

ARTHUR: No.

KATE: I keep forgetting you're all a generation beyond me.

ARTHUR: Yer not that much older than us.

KATE: I'm thirty-four, Arthur.

ARTHUR: Ye don't look it.

KATE: I feel it, and more.

ARTHUR: Why'd you never get married, Kate? Are all the fellas roun' you way deaf, dumb and blind or what? . . . Sorry, I'm speakin' outa turn . . .

KATE: It's not that I've never been asked, Arthur, it's just that . . . I'm not sure what I want . . . or who I want . . .

ARTHUR: My sister Mary's like you, over thirty an' not married an' in no hurry neither. My da goes spare about it. 'There's niver been no oul maids in our family' he keeps tellin' her, as if she's stayin' single just to annoy him, like . . . sorry . . . I don't mean I think you're an oul maid, Kate . . . it's just the way my da talks . . . my da's stupid . . . our Mary says if she can't have Clint Eastwood she doesn't want nobody . . . If you could have any-body ye wanted, who would it be?

KATE: Donald Sutherland.

ARTHUR: Who?

KATE: Donald Sutherland. He's a very famour actor. One of my favourite films is the one he made with Julie Christie. 'Don't Look Now' it was called.

ARTHUR: Never seen it.

KATE: I've seen it three times. Once in the cinema. Twice on television.

ARTHUR: What's it about?

KATE: Love . . . and death . . . there's a scene in it where they make love in an apartment in Venice . . . it's un-believably beautiful . . . tender . . . erotic . . . perfect . . . everything we all want.

ARTHUR: Hung like a horse is he?

KATE: What?

ARTHUR: Dead good-lookin' is he?

KATE: I think so . . . (*Then realising that* ARTHUR *is obliquely referring to his scarred appearance.*) But a lot of people don't find him attractive at all . . . beauty is in the eye of the beholder . . .

ARTHUR: So my ma keeps tellin' me . . . See ye later . . .

He exits.

KATE: My mother keeps telling me I'm not getting any younger, and if I don't make a decision soon about Roger Elliott M.D. he's going to find himself someone else . . . someone younger who will devote herself to providing the home and family he says he wants . . . she never asks what I want. She just hopes that this job is some sort of aberration I'll grow out of before my child-bearing years are over . . . (*She lifts the dictaphone.*) Dear Mother, I know I'm running out of time . . . nobody knows that more than me . . . more and more, I find myself looking at babies in prams, knowing I don't want to waken up some day to the realisation that I've left it too late. Men can have babies till the day they die, but not women. It's not fair . . . I want a baby and I don't want to get married and I don't have the courage to have a child alone. (*She sets the machine down.*) There's never been no oul maids in my family, Arthur . . . nor no unmarried mothers either . . . and the only man who ever touched me the way Donald Sutherland touched Julie Christie was committed to violence, and I sent him away.

She lifts the tape again, wipes her words away.

In the hairdressing section, SANDRA *is cutting* TOMMY's *hair.*

SANDRA: You know somethin' Tommy, your hair's a brilliant colour. Sorta blue-black like Superman's.

TOMMY (*pleased*): Do you think so?

SANDRA: Aye . . . pity ye haven't got the body to go along with the hair.

TOMMY: All-American white . . .

SANDRA: I was talkin' about muscles, not colour. You're too touchy you, do ye know that? What's wrong with your

da bein' an Indian? My da's a cowboy,
an' it doesn't bother me.

TOMMY: He wasn't an Indian.

SANDRA: Well what was he then?

TOMMY: I dunno . . . my mother doesn't
talk about it . . . she doesn't need to,
everybody round here does enough
talkin' for her.

SANDRA: Tommy, people round here
don't talk about you because you
might be a half-caste, they talk about
you because you're *definitely* an eejit.
Ye go on all the time as if ye'd
swallowed a dictionary or somethin'.

TOMMY: A prophet without honour . . .

SANDRA: What?

TOMMY: Karl Marx had to leave the
country of his birth.

SANDRA: Was he your da?

TOMMY: You take nuthin' serious.

SANDRA: I take a lotta things serious,
but you're not one of them.

TOMMY: You're as bad as the rest of
them round here. You make jokes
when somebody tries to tell you the
history of your own country.

SANDRA: I got enough of that at school.

TOMMY: I don't mean the great religious
political con. I mean the true history
of the division of the workin' classes
by the owners, the capitalists.

SANDRA: Listen you. Every mornin' I
get outa bed an' I look outa the
window an' the soldiers is still there.
That's all the history I need to know.

TOMMY: You need to know why they're
there.

SANDRA: I don't, Tommy. I just want
them to go away.

TOMMY: My mother says it's all God's
will an' it'll pass. She believes everything's God's will, includin' me. It's
how she copes.

SANDRA: Maybe yer da was an angel,

Tommy. Maybe you were one of then
virgin births . . . there's about one a
year on this road . . . God knows how
many there are in the whole of Ireland.

TOMMY: Angels are fair-skinned and
blue-eyed.

SANDRA: Says who?

TOMMY: Have you ever seen a small
brown angel with blue-black hair in a
stained-glass window?

SANDRA: You don't believe in all that
Tommy. You're a communist. It
shouldn't bother ye.

TOMMY: It doesn't bother me.

SANDRA *makes a disbelieving face
behind* TOMMY's *head.* ARTHUR
comes in.

SANDRA: Hey, Arthur, you want yer
head shaved?

ARTHUR: You off the knitting machines?

SANDRA: Mine's broke. I'm fillin' in the
time till they let me work on the cars.

ARTHUR: You should stick to the hair-
dressin' Sandra, yer dead good at it.

SANDRA: Friggin' waste of time. They
can't teach me nuthin' here I don't
know already. I've always done
everybody's hair in our house.

ARTHUR: When my hair grows will ye
streak it for me?

SANDRA: Your hair's never gonna grow.
Hair doesn't sprout through a steel
plate.

TOMMY: It'll grow roun' it. Like one of
them climbin' plants. You can put a
wee trellis on yer head Arthur an'
train it, like an ivy.

ARTHUR: The surgeon says it'll take a
year or two. I don't want it to grow
yet anyway. I hafta go intil the court
scarred limpin' an' bald to get the big
compensation.

SANDRA: It'll never grow.

ARTHUR: I'm a skinhead, I don't care.

SANDRA: You're a chancer. Skinheads shave their hair off on purpose. Yours got shot off by the army.

TOMMY: Did you know that the white men were the first to take scalps off the Indians? The Indians only copied what they done first. I read it in a magazine.

SANDRA: It's knowin' things like that gets ye a job.

TOMMY: I'm only sayin'.

SANDRA: Will ye sit still or ye'll end up scalped.

ARTHUR: I don't remember gettin' hit. I was walkin' down the street an' all of a sudden there was all this gunfire. A wee lad about that high run past me, an' I thought, you wee bugger you nearly got me shot. An' then I looked down an' there was all this blood, an' I thought, Christ, some poor bugger *has* got shot. An' I looked aroun' an' there was nobody there but me. An' then I fainted. There was no pain nor nuthin'. That come after.

TOMMY: If that had happened anywhere else in the British Isles you woulda died. Lucky fer you it happened here.

SANDRA: Will you sit still.

TOMMY: There are surgeons here what are the best in the world at puttin' broken bodies together. I read it in a magazine.

SANDRA: They get a lotta practice here, thanks til the terrorists.

TOMMY: An' the army an' the police. (*As if he's quoting from a text book.*) Terrorists only exist because of corrupt governments.

SANDRA: Listen dick-head, if somebody gets blowed to bits, what does it matter who done it, or why they done it?

ARTHUR: It matters if yer lookin' compensation.

TOMMY: If ye never ask why, yer never gonna change nuthin'.

SANDRA: I'm forever askin' why I'm stuck in this hole. Askin' changes nuthin'.

ARTHUR: When I get my compensation I could change yer life for yer Sandra.

SANDRA: Don't hold yer breath.

She walks off.

ARTHUR: She really fancies me, you know. It's only a matter of time.

TOMMY: Wee Oliver says you fancy Kate.

ARTHUR: Wee Oliver's head is fulla white mice.

TOMMY: You've no chance there, Arthur. Kate's doin' a line with a rich doctor up in the City Hospital, drives a big flash Volvo, so he does.

ARTHUR: How would you know?

TOMMY: Friend of mine, works there.

ARTHUR: Oh aye, brain surgeon is he?

TOMMY: No, he's one of the real workers. Cleans up the blood and guts after Kate's fancyman has finished cuttin' up the dead bodies.

ARTHUR (*grabbing hold of* TOMMY): Take that back!

TOMMY: It's true. He does the post mortems.

ARTHUR: He's not her fancyman. She's no tart.

TOMMY: They've been knockin' round together fer years, and he's doin' a line on the quiet with one of the nurses as well.

ARTHUR: You're a lyin' hound.

TOMMY: They're puttin' bets on in the hospital about how long he can keep the two of them goin' without Kate findin' out . . . maybe we should do her a favour an' tell her . . .

ARTHUR: I'm warnin' you. You say one word of that shite gossip to Kate an' *you'll* end up on a slab in the City Hospital.

TOMMY: All right! All right! Keep yer hair on.

ARTHUR: Ye made it all up, didn't ye? Didn't ye?

TOMMY: I'm away to get some fegs . . . (*He moves off.*) Are ye comin'?

ARTHUR: Some of us have work to do.

TOMMY exits. ARTHUR goes to KATE's desk where she is sitting writing. As he approaches, she sets down the pen and sighs.

ARTHUR: You all right, Kate?

KATE: I'm bored, Arthur. Bored out of my mind writing reports, filling in forms and trying to make sense of official letters. I seem to spend more and more time sitting in here, and less and less out there with you lot.

ARTHUR: You spend a lot of time with us.

KATE: Not enough.

ARTHUR: My sister was on a trainin' scheme for over six months an' she says she only clapped eyes on the man what run it once. An' even then somebody had to tell her he was the boss.

KATE: The boss . . . is that how you all see me?

ARTHUR: Well . . . that's what ye are.

KATE: What do they really think of me, Arthur? The kids out there? Sorry, I shouldn't ask you a question like that.

ARTHUR: They think yer dead-on.

KATE: But they're never completely at ease with me, are they? They don't chat to me the way they do with their section heads, the people who actually teach them how to repair cars and make things.

ARTHUR: Ach, that's because they know all themens. They're from roun' here, same as us.

KATE: And I'm not the same as you, am I? I don't speak the same language.

ARTHUR: You speak dead nice. You wouldn't wanta be like one of them pain-in-the-arse social workers what put the Belfast accent on, would ye? Ye can spot them a mile off. All training shoes an' black leather jackets. They think rollin' their own fegs and wearing' dirty jeans makes them one of the people. They're a joke. Nobody takes them serious. You're all right Kate. You don't try to be what yer not.

KATE: You know what I am Arthur? I'm a bored middle-class female who got excited by the civil rights movement in the sixties, and was so terrified by the violence that erupted around us when we marched from Belfast to Derry in the name of equal opportunities for all that I stopped marching, stopped protesting, and kidded myself that by getting a degree in social studies I could change the system from within. And here I am, fifteen years later, one of the bosses.

ARTHUR: We could do with more bosses like you.

KATE: When I was your age, Arthur, I believed there shouldn't be any bosses.

ARTHUR: That's oul commie talk. That's fer people like Tommy. Not fer people like you, Kate.

KATE: You know what I am, Arthur? A shadow of a socialist. The only difference between me and Donal Davoren is that I'm bluffing nobody but myself.

Offstage the teenagers chant. (ARTHUR *goes off to join them.*)

FIRST VOICE:
No job, nothing to do
No money, on the Bru   Repeat

SECOND VOICE:
No job after school
No future that's the rule   Repeat

ALL: Unemployment. Unemployment.

THIRD VOICE:
'O' Levels. 'A' Levels. 'X' 'Y' 'Z' Levels.
'O' Levels. 'A' Levels. 'X' 'Y' 'Z' Levels.

ALL: Unemployment. Unemployment.

(*Then a mixture of all the chants simultaneously rising in volume.*) KATE *puts her hands over her ears. Shouts 'Stop!'*

Scene Four

Mid-March. SANDRA *and* MAUREEN *enter, followed by* TOMMY.

SANDRA: You told Johnnie's probation officer? Are ye out of yer friggin' mind?

She begins to do MAUREEN's *hair.* TOMMY *sits watching and reading a magazine.*

MAUREEN: I didn't know what else to to. I don't want him put away. I can't watch him all the time. When I'm here I never know if he's at school or roamin' the streets. She's nice, Claudia. She cares what happens til us.

SANDRA: She cares about keepin' her job. They all do.

MAUREEN: No, she's different, like Kate.

SANDRA: A do-gooder.

KATE *comes in, listens. They don't see her.*

TOMMY: Doin' her bit fer the poor. It's her job.

MAUREEN: She does a whole lot more for us she doesn't get paid fer doin'.

TOMMY: An' then goes back til her posh house up the Malone Road. If she's so liberated, why does she still live there with her ma instead of roun' here like us.

KATE: Because I'm lazy, that's why. My mother runs the house, and that leaves me free to run this place. It suits both of us.

MAUREEN: There's nuthin' wrong with livin' in a nice house. You mind yer own business, Tommy.

SANDRA: How many lives in your house, Kate?

KATE: Just the two of us. My father's dead. My two brothers are married.

SANDRA: I wish some of our ones would go off an' get married. There's ten of us an' three bedrooms. Ye can call nuthin' yer own.

TOMMY: If Arthur wins ask him to buy ye a big house in the country.

MAUREEN: I wonder how he's gettin' on?

TOMMY' It'll be all over by now. Sorry son, if the army says you were joyridin' that's good enough for us. No compensation.

KATE: He has a good case, you know. That solicitor wouldn't have taken him on if he hadn't thought he might win.

TOMMY: Sure, they get paid anyway, win or lose or draw. They'll take anybody on.

ARTHUR *comes in. He is wearing a suit.* SANDRA *and* TOMMY *fall about laughing.*

SANDRA: Frig, get him. Man from C an' A.

TOMMY: Where did ye get that outfit?

SANDRA: His ma's been shoplifting again.

KATE: Leave him alone you lot. You look very nice Arthur.

SANDRA: He looks like a tailor's dummy.

TOMMY: He looks like yer man, Yorkie.

KATE: Who's Yorkie?

SANDRA: The Secretary of State. Big, rich an' thick. Well, you're big an' yer thick, Arthur, but are ye rich?

ARTHUR *says nothing. Slowly takes off his tie.*

TOMMY: I knew ye wouldn't get nuthin'.

SANDRA: He's smirkin'. He got somethin'.

TOMMY: Did ye?

SANDRA: Look at his face.

ARTHUR: You are now lookin' at the most illegible bachelor in West Belfast.

TOMMY: How much did ye get?

ARTHUR *takes twenty Benson & Hedges from his pocket. (Normally the teenagers have tens of cheap cigarettes.) He slowly counts out five cigarettes onto a table.*

MAUREEN: Five . . . five hundred pounds?

TOMMY: You got yer costs.

ARTHUR *shakes his head. Places another two cigarettes on the table.*

SANDRA: Jeesus, he got seven thousand. (ARTHUR *grins.*) Ye did, didn't ye?

ARTHUR *shakes his head.*

SANDRA: Well, what then?

ARTHUR: I got seventy. (*There is a stunned silence.*) Seventy friggin' thousand pounds!

TOMMY: I don't believe ye.

SANDRA: Yer a lyin' hound.

ARTHUR: Hand on my heart an' hope to die.

MAUREEN: It's a fortune.

KATE: Well done, Arthur.

ARTHUR: I done nuthin'. It was the solicitor. He was brilliant, like the fella in the big picture. I mean it was all dead borin' at first, statements from witnesses an' hospital reports fulla big words. I couldn't make out the half of it, an' then the oul solicitor gets up and tells the court about the oul steel plate an' the hair not growin' an' the headaches, an' how my social life's ruined with the scars an' the limp . . . I never let on you were mad about me anyway, Sandra . . . I tell ye, he was that good he nearly had me in tears, I was that sorry fer myself.

MAUREEN: Seventy thousand pounds.

ARTHUR: I always hoped I'd get somethin', a couple of thousand maybe, an' then the day when I heard him talkin' I thought, they're gonna give me more, maybe ten, an' then the judge said seventy . . . I thought I was friggin' hearin' things.

KATE: You deserve it, Arthur, every penny and more. It sounds like a lot of money, but it has to do you for a lifetime.

SANDRA: Where is it? The money? Are Securicar waitin' at the front door?

ARTHUR: They don't give ye the loot in a suitcase, Sandra. You're as bad as my da. He thought he was gonna walk out of the court like Al Capone. Seventy G's in used notes.

TOMMY: Do they give ye a cheque or what?

ARTHUR: They give me nuthin'. It goes intil a trust till my eighteenth birthday.

SANDRA: There's always a catch.

ARTHUR: That's what my da said. You shoulda seen his face when he heard he wasn't gettin' his hands on it. When we come outa the court he puts his arm roun' my shoulders an' he says, 'Arthur son, you'll see me an' your mother right, won't ye? All them sleepless nights we sat up in the hospital prayin' for ye.' My ma sat up in the hospital, he did his prayin' in the pub. I never remember my da puttin' his arm roun' me before the day.

TOMMY: It's a wonder he let ye out of his sight.

SANDRA: Did they not give ye nuthin' in advance?

ARTHUR: No.

SANDRA: Frig. I never thought ye'd get it, but I thought if ye did we'd all get a drink outa it anyway.

KATE: I knew he'd win.

She produces a bottle of champagne from her bag.

ARTHUR: Is that real?

KATE: The real McCoy.

SANDRA: Where'd ye nick it?

KATE: The Forum Hotel. I won it, at a supper dance.

MAUREEN: In a raffle like?

KATE: Tombola. I think you should open it, Arthur.

ARTHUR: I've always wanted to open a bottle of champagne.

KATE: You just turn this until the cork comes up . . .

SANDRA: Here, it pops out, doesn't it? Quick, Maureen, cups. Arthur, wait a minute it'll spill all over the place.

MAUREEN *and* SANDRA *run to the kitchen, get cups, the cork pops. They catch the champagne.*

KATE: To Arthur.

TEENAGERS: Arthur!

They taste it.

TOMMY: So that's what it's like.

MAUREEN: It's different from what I thought . . .

SANDRA: It's diabolical.

ARTHUR: I like it.

SANDRA: They seen ye comin' Kate. It's like fizzy dishwater.

TOMMY: Somebody gettin' rid of their oul cheap muck in a raffle.

ARTHUR: I like it.

KATE: Actually it is one of the best champagnes.

MAUREEN: Like the pop stars drink?

KATE: Yes.

ARTHUR: I like it.

TOMMY: What does it cost, if ye were buyin' it?

KATE: Around twenty pounds a bottle.

SANDRA: Yer friggin' jokin'.

ARTHUR: I knew it was good. It's like the difference between saute potatoes an' chips.

SANDRA: Saute potatoes *is* chips, undercooked.

ARTHUR: No it's not.

SANDRA: Yes it is, unless you're doin' it wrong. An' somebody puttin' a fancy name on it doesn't make it better, just different an' more dear.

TOMMY (*admiringly*): Sandra, I wish you would join the Party.

SANDRA: What for? To end up typin' letters fer wankers like you?

MAUREEN: It gets nicer, the more ye drink.

ARTHUR: Could anybody lend us a fiver till pay day? Only I would like to buy yiz all a drop of what ye fancy.

SANDRA: Seventy thousand friggin' quid, and he's lookin' a sub fer a six pack.

MAUREEN: What are ye gonna do with all that money, Arthur?

ARTHUR: I have plans, baby, I have plans.

KATE: Have you any plans for tonight?

SANDRA: It's Wednesday, nobody roun' here has any readies on a Wednesday.

TOMMY: Arthur's credit'll be good in the pub. His da'll be drinkin' on the slate already on the strength of what's to come.

KATE: Do you fancy coming up to my house, the four of you? I'll supply the drinks and Arthur can cook the supper.

SANDRA: Your house?

KATE: Yes. (*There is an awkward pause.*) It was just a thought.

MAUREEN: I'd like to go.

TOMMY: Your ma wouldn't want the likes of us in your house.

KATE: My mother's staying with her

sister for a few days.

MAUREEN: You all on yer own like, Kate?

KATE: Look, you don't have to . . . I just said it on the spur of the moment . . .

ARTHUR: You got a big posh kitchen, Kate?

KATE: Yes.

ARTHUR: An' ye'd let me cook in it?

KATE: I'd love you to cook in it, I hate cooking.

ARTHUR: Yer on. Can I cook anything I want?

KATE: Within reason.

TOMMY: What had ye in mind?

ARTHUR: It'll be a surprise.

SANDRA: Your food's always a friggin' surprise.

ARTHUR: Ye don' have to come if ye don't want to.

SANDRA: Might as well. I've nuthin' better to do.

KATE: Tommy? You want to see how the other half live?

TOMMY: I know how the other half live.

SANDRA: He read it in a magazine.

TOMMY: Have you got a library?

KATE: I've got a lot of books.

TOMMY: Can I look at them?

SANDRA: He wants to colour in the pictures.

KATE: Of course you can look at them.

SANDRA: Don't lend him none, he'll flog them.

MAUREEN: What time'll we come, only I'll hafta make our Johnnie his tea first.

SANDRA: Why can't the wee bugger make his own tea?

KATE: Whatever time you like. Oh, and Arthur, you'll need money to buy in the ingredients for the surprise meal. Do you mind? I'll be here still after

six. I won't have time to go shopping. (*She hands him some money.*) You'd better go now before the supermarket closes.

SANDRA: I'm goin' with him, he'll go mad an' buy a lot of oul daft rubbish.

ARTHUR: Hey Sandra, I've always wanted to push a trolley roun' the supermarket with you.

SANDRA: Well, enjoy it the day. It'll be the first an' last time.

They exit.

TOMMY: Do you want me to get you some booze Kate? Only I know a place where you can get it cheap.

KATE: Eh, no thanks Tommy, I have some at home.

TOMMY: Next time yer stockin' up, give us a shout.

He exits.

MAUREEN: Do you know what must be the best thing about having money? Never havin' to go to the Social Security. I hate that place. Do you think I'll get a job when my time's up here?

KATE: You're hard working, conscientious, no police record. You have a high chance.

MAUREEN: You've no chance when the Job Centre finds out yer from Divis Flats.

KATE: I'm hoping to organise a typing course. Would you like to do it?

MAUREEN: Me work in an office?

KATE: Why not?

MAUREEN: The only office work I'm likely to get is washin' floors.

KATE: You can do better than that.

MAUREEN: It wouldn't bother me. I just want a job. Any sort of a job. I don't care what it is. I wanta earn my own money, never stand in no more queues pleadin' poverty. Never have to fill in no more forms. 'Where's

your father? — I don't know. Where's
your mother? — In the looney bin.'
I'll spend a year here and at the end of
it I'll be back where I started off. No
job, no money. Arthur spends a year
in the hospital, an' at the end of it he
gets seventy thousand pounds . . . I
wonder would the army like to shoot
me?

Pause.

*Offstage the song 'Children of Divis
Flats'*

Blackout.

ACT TWO

Scene One

KATE's *house after the meal.* ARTHUR
sings 'Oh I was out walking'.

ARTHUR (*sings straight*): Oh I was out
walking outside Divis Flats
Where the happiest tenants are surely
the rats
Where we all breathe asbestos and
no one is well
I walked down the steps and I tripped
and I fell
And I never knew when I had my fall
The Executive owned the steps, and
the D.O.E. owned the wall

I was took to the doctor all aching and
sore
My ankle is swollen, can't walk
anymore
He gave me some tablets and we had
a talk
They made me feel dizzy, I still
cannot walk.

ALL: And he never knew, when I had my
fall
The Executive owned the steps, and
the D.O.E. owned the wall.

ARTHUR (*parodying the worst type of
Irish nasal country and western singer*):
My mother was raging, she went for a
claim
She looked up a number and solicitor's
name
She told him my story and he was all
ears
But he shook his head sadly 'This
claim will take years'

ALL: Pity he didn't know when he had
his fall
The Executive owned the steps, and
the D.O.E. the wall.

ARTHUR: It's now five years later, and
the claim's still not paid
There's wrangles and tangles, no
settlement made
There's 'phone calls and letters, they
argue and talk

I'm stuck in the flat now; I still cannot walk.

ALL: And nobody cares about you at all
When the Executive owns the steps,
and the D.O.E. owns the wall.

And nobody cares about you at all
When the Executive owns the steps,
and the D.O.E. owns the wall.

They all cheer, applaud. KATE *and* ARTHUR *go off to the kitchen.*

MAUREEN: It was lovely, wasn't it. Arthur's awful good at the cookin'.

SANDRA: Do ye want more wine?

MAUREEN: Leave some fer Kate an' Arthur.

TOMMY: Plenty more where that come from. I wonder what the poor people are doin' these days?

SANDRA: I thought the party didn't approve of this sorta livin'.

TOMMY: We want everybody to live like this, not just the privileged few.

SANDRA: Oh aye? An' who's gonna do the dirty work while everybody's livin' like this?

TOMMY: Machines.

SANDRA: You've been readin' them star-wars comics again.

TOMMY: Some of the ornaments in this house would feed a family fer a fortnight. (*He picks up a photo in a silver frame.*) Here, look at this . . . to Kate, all my love, Roger. Must be her fella.

SANDRA: Give us a dekko . . . here, he's not bad lookin' . . . for a Roger.

MAUREEN: He's lovely lookin'.

SANDRA: A wee screw.

MAUREEN: You make everything cheap so ye do.

TOMMY: Nuthin' cheap about this place.

MAUREEN: Can the two of yiz not just enjoy yourselves. It's lovely here.

SANDRA: She'll be day dreamin' all day the morra.

MAUREEN: There's nuthin' wrong with day dreamin'.

SANDRA: There is if you believe in it. None of us is never gonna live nowhere but them stinkin' flats . . . unless we emigrate . . .

TOMMY: Nobody'd have us.

MAUREEN: If you could live anywhere in the world, where would ye go?

SANDRA: Dunno, but I'll tell ye where I wouldn't go, friggin' America. Once was enough.

MAUREEN: You don't know what side yer bread's buttered on. You got a free holiday, an' all ye ever done was complain about it. Half the school wanted to go, an' you were the one got picked.

SANDRA: I never had no luck.

MAUREEN: Vera Cosgrove went one year an' she thought it was brilliant.

SANDRA: Vera Cosgrove's a lick.

MAUREEN: I'm tryin' to get our Johnnie on one of them trips.

SANDRA: With his record? Are ye jokin'?

MAUREEN: They haven't said no yet.

TOMMY: They will. They only take the well-behaved deservin' poor.

MAUREEN: They must be considerin' him. They give me a whole lotta stuff to read.

She rummages in her bag, produces some leaflets.

TOMMY: Let me see . . . (*He reads.*) The Tennessee Summer Holiday Program for Irish Children . . . was that where you went, Sandra?

SANDRA: I was in North Carolina. Must be the most borin' place on God's earth. They never stop prayin'.

KATE *and* ARTHUR *come in carrying liqueurs.*

ARTHUR: I told Kate she'd get done fer aidin' an' abettin' under-age drinkin', but she says this is a special occasion.

KATE: And I'm running you all home afterwards to make sure you don't get picked up.

MAUREEN: It's lovely roun' here. No army nor police nor nuthin'.

TOMMY: No need. They don't make petrol bombs roun' here, just money.

SANDRA (*sniffing the liqueur*): What's this?

KATE: It's a coffee liqueur.

SANDRA *swallows a large mouthful, coughs, splutters.*

SANDRA: Jeesus!

ARTHUR: Yer supposed to sip it slow, ye ignoramous.

MAUREEN (*sipping hers*): It's lovely.

SANDRA: It beats glue.

KATE: Do you sniff glue, Sandra?

SANDRA: Nigh an' again.

KATE: Why?

SANDRA: Why do flies eat shite?

TOMMY: Because they can't afford gin and tonic.

KATE: Do you all do it?

ARTHUR: I usta. After the accident I never bothered no more.

SANDRA: He's afraid it'll rust the oul steel plate.

MAUREEN: I never done it. It's the road to nowhere.

SANDRA: You never do nuthin'. That's why yer so miserable all the time.

TOMMY *is reading the leaflets about America.*

TOMMY: You'd think we were refugees. Have you read these, Maureen?

MAUREEN: Only some of them. I only got them the day.

TOMMY: Listen to this . . . 'You will love America. You will be coming to a peaceful place, a happy place, a safe place. No rioting, no shooting, no bombs, no soldiers.'

SANDRA: No hope . . .

TOMMY: 'Things you should know about the American people . . . '

SANDRA: When they're not talkin' they're eatin'.

TOMMY: 'Americans bathe or shower regularly, at least several times a week, or even every day. Your hosts will expect you to do this too. You will find American showers a lot of fun.'

SANDRA: See what I mean? They think we're still washin' under the pump in the yard.

TOMMY (*reading from the leaflet*): An' they think we might not of heard of foods like baked potatoes, mustard, cucumber an' spaghetti . . .

KATE: Let me see that. What is it?

SANDRA: Free holidays fer the poor an' needy.

KATE (*reading*): 'In America we call baps, dinner rolls . . .' Is this a joke?

SANDRA: It's a friggin' insult.

KATE (*reading*): Many Americans are of Irish descent, so you will find some familiar foods such as spam and Campbells Scotch Broth.'

SANDRA *pretends to be sick.*

ARTHUR: My ma says they usta send food parcels over here durin' the war. Now they're taking the kids over there to eat their leftovers.

KATE: We'll have to send you over, Arthur. Teach them how to cook.

SANDRA: When I was in America, the Bible-thumper I stopped with says one day . . . little girl, we are going to give you a special treat. We're taking you to a real Chinese restaurant.

Won't that be exciting? She got all huffed when I told her that we've more friggin' Chinese restaurants than chip shops in Belfast. An' anyway, I hate Chinese food.

ARTHUR: I didn't see you turnin' up yer nose at my sweet an' sour pork the night.

SANDRA: I knew what was in it. I was with ye when ye bought the stuff. See in them restaurants? They cook dogs an' cats an' dead pigeons, so they do.

MAUREEN: They do not.

SANDRA: They do, it's a well-known fact.

TOMMY: I'll tell ye somthin' that's not a well-known fact . . .

SANDRA: The Pope's doin' a line with Maggie Thatcher.

ARTHUR: What's the fastest thing on two wheels?

SANDRA: The Pope ridin' up the Shankill on a bicycle. What's the fastest thing on two legs?

ARTHUR: Ian Paisley runnin' after him.

TOMMY: What language is spoken by most of the people in Ireland?

SANDRA: Are you talkin' or chewin' a brick or what Tommy?

ARTHUR: I dunno that one.

TOMMY: It's not a stupid joke. It's a question. What do most people speak here?

ARTHUR: English.

TOMMY: An' what's the next language what most people speak here?

SANDRA: Jail Irish.

TOMMY: No, not even school Irish.

ARTHUR: What then?

TOMMY: Chinese.

ARTHUR: Yer head's cut.

TOMMY: It's true.

ARTHUR: How do ye know?

SANDRA: Picked his nose an' it fell out.

TOMMY: I read it in a magazine. There are so many Chinese restaurants here that Chinese is the second language of Ireland. Do ye not think that's an' amazin' fact?

SANDRA: No.

TOMMY: I don't understand you, Sandra.

SANDRA: You don't understand me?

TOMMY: Yer bright an' yer stupid all at the same time.

SANDRA: An' you were definitely a forceps delivery.

TOMMY: An' you were born up an entry.

SANDRA: At least I know who my da is.

MAUREEN (*screams*): Stop it. Tell them to stop it, Kate!

They all stare at her.

KATE: Maureen?

MAUREEN: They're spoilin' it. They always spoil it . . . everything nice . . . makin' a joke of it . . . makin' it rotten . . . I don't like dirty talk . . . yiz spoil everything so ye do . . .

She runs out. KATE goes after her. There is silence for a moment.

TOMMY: What's up with her these days? Every time you look roun' she's cryin' about somthin'.

SANDRA: It's that head-the-ball Johnnie. If he was my brother I'd kick his friggin' head in.

ARTHUR: People keep kickin' his head in. It makes no difference.

TOMMY: He's addicted til it. He wasn't even ten the first time he went joyridin'. Him an' another wee lad. They were that small, one of them had til turn the steerin' wheel, while the other one worked the foot pedals. An oul green van it was. They drove it intil a brick wall an' scarpered. The wall an' the car was wrecked, an' they got out without a mark on them.

SANDRA: Jammy wee buggers.

ARTHUR: There'll be more than a mark on him if the Provos get the houl of him. They gave Frankie Devlin a terrible hammerin'.

TOMMY: They wouldn't do that to Johnnie. He's only twelve.

SANDRA: It's freelance thieves they're beatin' up these days. You'd better start stealin' for them instead of for yerself Tommy, or ye'll be gettin' yer knees broke with the hurley bat.

KATE *comes back with* MAUREEN.

MAUREEN: I'm sorry. I dunno what got intil me. I musta drunk that liqueur too quick.

There is an awkward silence.

KATE: Shall I make some coffee;

MAUREEN: I'll hafta go soon. The woman next door said she'd keep an eye on Johnnie, but she goes to bed early so she does. I don't wanta spoil yer night out. I'll go home on the bus.

KATE: You'll do nothing of the sort. It's time we were all going.

ARTHUR: Aye, I need my beauty sleep.

SANDRA: You need a body transplant.

MAUREEN: We never done the dishes or nuthin' Kate.

KATE: There's no need. We have a dishwasher.

ARTHUR: We have a dishwasher in our house too. My granny.

SANDRA: Ha friggin' ha.

KATE: Come on, let's go.

MAUREEN: It was lovely Kate, thanks very much.

KATE, MAUREEN *and* TOMMY *exit.*
SANDRA *goes to follow them, stops, drains a couple of glasses.*

ARTHUR: Sandra?

SANDRA: What?

ARTHUR: Put it back.

SANDRA: What?

ARTHUR: Put it back.

SANDRA: Ye want me to spit it intil the bottle?

ARTHUR: The bottle in yer bag. Put it back.

SANDRA: What bottle?

ARTHUR: I seen ye, earlier on.

SANDRA: They put eyes in the back of yer head up in the hospital?

ARTHUR: Put it back.

SANDRA: They'll never miss it.

ARTHUR: You don't steal from yer own.

SANDRA: She's not one of us.

ARTHUR: She's as near as makes no difference.

SANDRA: She's a pain.

ARTHUR: She's a lady.

SANDRA: An' you're plannin' to be a gentleman now yer rich?

ARTHUR: Put it back.

SANDRA: You know the only reason you got the compensation? 'Cause you've got no record. An' that's only because you never got caught. You're no better than me.

ARTHUR: I never said I was.

SANDRA: You fancy her. You do, don't ye?

ARTHUR: Put the bottle back.

SANDRA *takes the bottle from her bag. Puts it on the table.*

SANDRA: Put it back yerself.

ARTHUR *replaces the bottle.*

SANDRA: Honest Arthur the boss's friend. You'll be gettin' religion next.

ARTHUR: You'll be gettin' jail next time yer caught.

SANDRA: What's that to you?

ARTHUR: Nuthin'.

SANDRA: If I do you can always bail me

out with all that money yer gettin'.

ARTHUR *grabs her. Kisses her clumsily. She pushes him away.*

SANDRA: Get off, scarface.

She walks out. ARTHUR *stands, looking slightly forlorn for a moment, then shrugs.*

ARTHUR: Cheeky get.

He looks around the room.

ARTHUR: Won't be long til I can afford a place like this.

SONG

Damp, Damp, Damp, Damp, Damp, Damp, Damp, Damp.

Mushrooms on my ceiling, drips on the wall
Steaming soaking bedclothes, blackened flaky halls
Spiders on the woodwork, mould on the clothes
Children lying in the beds, they're nearly froze.

I went to the Housing Executive, to explain my situation
I said 'I've got terrible damp'
They said 'It's only condensation'.

No, it's damp, damp, damp, damp, damp, damp, damp, damp.

Toilets overflowing, carpets all wet
If you think that's bad, take a look at that.

It's rats, rats, rats, rats, rats, rats, rats, rats.

Rats will bite your nose off, then just slink away
They're living in our bedrooms, they are here to stay.
Rats are full of poison, carry germs and fleas
You don't know what you could catch — some horrible disease.
Old Mother Hubbard went to the cupboard to get a piece of bread
She put her hand in the breadbin, and

found something else instead
AUGH!
She found rats, rats, rats, rats, rats, rats, rats, rats.
They bring their families with them for breakfast, lunch and tea
I am paying heat and rent, but they are living free.

Every little tiny rat is out to get your child and cat!

Damp, damp, damp, damp, damp, damp, damp, damp.

Scene Two

The Lagan Mill. End of March.

KATE, *sitting reading an official letter. She phones* CLAUDIA.

KATE: Hello Claudia? It's Kate, look I'm sorry, but I can't meet you for lunch today, I've a meeting with the hierarchy later this morning, and I've been asked to partake of a civil service lunch afterwards. Cold cuts and cheap white wine to cushion the bribe . . . I'm being manipulated into having an open day. You know the sort of thing — important official comes in, swans around making patronising comments about the kids' work, pats them all on their dear little well-scrubbed heads, and hopefully goes off feeling righteous enough to recommend funding for another year . . . no, of course I know it's not ultimately up to me . . . it's just that I would like to have the courage to say 'Stuff your open day and your pompous V.I.P. I will not have the kids here paraded out like a chimps' tea party. Give them the bloody money as a right not a privilege for good behaviour.' But I won't. I'll make the nominal protest, which will be noted in the minutes (black mark, Kate) and then I'll be grown up and reasonable and will organise the event to perfection (gold star, Kate) . . . Claudia, you don't have to justify my reasons for agreeing. I've become very

adept at doing that for myself. I'm
just saying out loud what I want to
do, before I agree to what I have to
do . . . God, isn't it a long time since
we sang 'We Shall Overcome' and
believed it . . . Listen, do you fancy
going to the Opera House this evening?
I've got complimentary tickets, and
Roger's working late. Oh . . . no, no,
it's all right I'll take mother . . . have
a good time. I'll give you a call next
week . . . Thanks, bye.

She replaces the receiver. SANDRA
comes in. KATE *looks at her watch.*

KATE: I don't believe it. Were you up
all night?

SANDRA: We were all up all night. They
got Tommy. Four o'clock this mornin'.

KATE: Who got Tommy?

SANDRA: The great lads he's always
bummin' he's so friendly with.

KATE: What happened?

SANDRA: They broke both his hands.
Stupid bugger. I warned him, we all
did. You don't steal round here. You
do it in the big shops in the town.
They don't mind that.

KATE: They broke his hands?

SANDRA: They'da done worse, only his
ma run intil the street, squealin'.
Next thing the army was in. They used
it as an excuse to take the flats apart.
You wanna see the state of the place.
Glass everywhere.

KATE: There was nothing about it on the
news this morning.

SANDRA: Our windows is always gettin'
broke. It's not news. Who cares about
the army smashin' up the windows and
the doors in Divis Flats. The bloody
place is fallin' to bits anyway. Walls
streamin' with water, toilets over-
flowin', rubbish chutes that don't
work. If the rats an' the bugs don't
get ye, the asbestos will . . . or the
police, or the army, or the I.R.A. . . .
who cares?

KATE: Did you see Tommy?

SANDRA: No. But I heard him. Pigs!
An' they're supposed to be on our
side.

KATE: Sandra, you're worn out. Go back
home and get some sleep.

SANDRA: And get my pay docked? Are
you jokin'? I'm down the best part of
a pound already this week.

MAUREEN *comes in.*

MAUREEN: Did she tell you?

KATE: Yes. Did you see Tommy?

MAUREEN: Johnnie an' me hid under
the bed till it was all over.

SANDRA: Did they not come in til your
place?

MAUREEN: Somebody hammered on
the door, but we never let on ourselves
an' they went away.

SANDRA: Couldn'ta been the Brits.
They'da broke the door down.

MAUREEN: Is Arthur not in yet? I'm
dyin' fer a cuppa tea. They've cut off
the water as well as the electric, Kate.

KATE: Who?

MAUREEN: It happens all the time.

SANDRA: Arthur got picked up.

MAUREEN: What for?

SANDRA: He came out onto the balcony
to see what was goin' on, an' they had
him in the back of the landrover
before his feet had time to touch the
ground.

KATE: He wasn't doing anything?

SANDRA: Jeesus, Kate, you might as
well live on the moon fer all ye know.
You don't have to be doin't nuthin'.
Ye just hafta be there. He's a stupid
get, Arthur. He's got picked up like
that before. One look at that face of
his an' they haul him in fer
questioning.

MAUREEN: It's not right.

SANDRA: His solicitor'll have him out before lunchtime. He's used to it. Can I make some tea Kate?

KATE: Yes, of course you can. I'll go and see who's in.

MAUREEN: There'll not be many in the day. They'll all be sleepin' or standin' aroun' talking about it . . .

KATE: Did anybody else from in here get picked up?

SANDRA: That wee lad Oliver from the joinery section. He was lobbin' milk bottles at the Brits. He got three of them before they grabbed him. He's dead good. He plays darts.

KATE: Anybody else?

SANDRA: Not from in here. The rest they lifted was on the dole. Can I make a bitta toast as well, Kate? Only I'm starvin'.

KATE: Yes.

She exits.

SANDRA: She takes it all dead serious, doesn't she? Do ye want toast, Maureen?

MAUREEN: No, just a cuppa tea.

SANDRA: How did ye keep your Johnnie in? He loves all that. Did ye nail his feet til the floor?

MAUREEN: I give him a pound.

SANDRA: Yer mad. He'll be out buyin' glue with it.

MAUREEN: He doesn't do that no more.

SANDRA: Like he doesn't joyride no more? Wise up, Maureen. He's wired to the friggin' moon that wee lad.

MAUREEN: You usta go in the back of the cars.

SANDRA: I grew out of it.

MAUREEN: Our Johnnie's grew out of it too. (SANDRA *gives her a long look*.) . . . I asked him why he keeps doin' it. He says it's a laugh.

SANDRA: It usta be a laugh. It stopped

bein' funny the day the Brits stopped shoutin' halt an' opened fire. Do ye know Geordie Quinn? They got him right there. (*She points to below her navel*.) He showed me his stitches. Another two inches an' he'd a got the D.S.O. Why do ye not want any toast?

MAUREEN: I'm not hungry.

SANDRA: You ate nuthin' these days. What's up with ye?

MAUREEN: What do ye mean?

SANDRA: Suit yerself. Aw frig, there's no milk.

MAUREEN: The crate's at the front door. I'll get it.

SANDRA: It's heavy. I'll get it.

There is a pause.

MAUREEN: What am I gonna do, Sandra?

SANDRA: What are ye askin' me for?

MAUREEN: You asked me. How did ye know?

SANDRA: I've two older sisters. I've seen that look. Candles to the virgin an' promises never to do it again. How far gone are ye?

MAUREEN: Four week an' three days.

SANDRA: You could still be all right.

MAUREEN: I went to Boots. I'm not all right.

SANDRA: Have ye told him?

MAUREEN: He's away home for a month. He's a student.

SANDRA: Away home where?

MAUREEN: I met him in the Botanic Gardens.

SANDRA: Where?

MAUREEN: The Botanic Gardens. It's behind the university.

SANDRA: I only know roun' here. What were ye doin' away over there?

MAUREEN: It's not far from the hospital. I go an' look at the plants sometimes. There's a palm house and a tropical ravine and the Ulster Museum. It's lovely. Ye should go sometime.

SANDRA: Is that where ye done it?

MAUREEN: He lives in a flat, roun' the corner. Not like our flats. In an old house with a garden. It's lovely.

SANDRA: Jeesus, you musta been at the back of the queue when they were handin' out the brains.

MAUREEN: What am I gonna do, Sandra?

SANDRA: How would I know?

MAUREEN: What would you do?

SANDRA: I don't do it. Nobody's never gonna catch me like that.

MAUREEN: I thought . . .

SANDRA: Ye thought what?

MAUREEN: Nuthin'.

SANDRA: You see fellas? They talk about ye if ye do it, an' they make it up if ye don't.

MAUREEN: They'll all talk about me.

SANDRA: This road's hivin' with kids. One more won't make no difference.

MAUREEN: It'll look different.

SANDRA: What way different?

MAUREEN: He's not from roun' here.

SANDRA: Tommy's da wasn't from roun' here. My ma says he was a half-caste what come roun' the doors sellin' floor polish. She says that's why Tommy has a bit of a tan all the year roun'.

MAUREEN: They'll take Johnnie away when they find out.

SANDRA: They're gonna take Johnnie away anyway . . . Has he any money, Cairo Fred or whoever he is? You can make him pay. It's the law.

MAUREEN: We only done it twice.

SANDRA: Once is enough. God but you're thick. I suppose he told you he loved you?

MAUREEN: He was lovely. He talks awful nice. Not like the ones round here (SANDRA *rolls her eyes in disbelief.*) I'll get the milk.

SANDRA: I'll get the friggin' milk. You rest yer swelled ankles.

MAUREEN: His father's a prince or somethin'.

SANDRA: Aye, an' Tommy's da was Omar Sharif.

She exits. MAUREEN *looks down.*

MAUREEN: There's nuthin' the matter with my ankles . . . (*She begins to work the knitting machine, stops, looks down.*) Don't heed her baby . . . he loves me . . . I know he does . . . he said he did . . . and he's a gentleman . . . (*She operates the knitting machine again, stops.*) We're gonna live in an old house behind the university . . . and every day I'll put you in your pram and wheel you round the Botanic Gardens . . . a proper pram . . . Silver Cross with big high wheels . . . and everybody'll look at you, you'll be that beautiful . . . your father's dark eyes an' your grannie's blonde hair . . . (*She stops at the thought of her mother.* SANDRA *comes in, sets the milk down, watches and listens to* MAUREEN *who doesn't see her.*) Your granny was like the sun . . . all golden . . . she lit up everything she touched . . . she come from the country and got cooped up in the flats like a battery hen . . . the day your granda went to England to look for work, we were that miserable she took me an' Johnnie to the pictures . . . The Wizard of Oz . . . it was lovely . . . an' the next day she bought seven pot plants . . . seven . . . an' she put them in a row on the kitchen window sill an' she said . . . 'They'll all flower except for the fourth one. That one has to stay green.' And she wouldn't tell us why. 'Wait and see' she said . . . 'Wait and see.' We watched an' we waited for a while an' nuthin' happened, an' we lost interest. Didn't even notice them anymore. And then one day I come in from school an' all the pot plants had flowers except the fourth one, just like she said. (*She smiles and counts on her fingers.*) Red, orange, yellow, green, blue, indigo, violet . . . 'See' she said, 'we have a rainbow on our window sill.' (*She looks round, sees* SANDRA.) You come in that day . . . do you remember?

SANDRA: You an' your Johnnie were dancin' round the kitchen singin' 'Somewhere over the rainbow' an' your mother was laughin' an' she said 'We're all mad in this family, Sandra. Some day the men in the white coats are gonna come in and take us all away.'

MAUREEN: Our Johnnie doesn't remember it. I asked him the other day.

SANDRA: It was a long time ago.

MAUREEN: He's the spittin' image of her. Blond curly hair, blue eyes. Like one of them cherubs in the stained-glass windows. How can he look so like her and be so different? She only had to smile at you and you felt warm . . . Johnnie's light doesn't warm . . . it burns . . . it burns . . . and I can't get anywhere near him . . . (*She is incoherent, sobbing.*) And I don't know what to do . . .

SANDRA: Maureen, don't, you'll make yourself sick . . .

MAUREEN: You mean mad . . . like her . . .

SANDRA: No I don't. Come on Maureen . . . into the loo . . . wash your face an' I'll make ye a cuppa tea . . . come on . . . you don't want anybody to see you like this . . . you know the way they talk . . . come on . . .

She looks as if she wants to touch MAUREEN, *but can't.* MAUREEN *walks, dazed, towards the exit, turns back to* SANDRA.

MAUREEN: Sure you won't tell nobody . . .

SANDRA: Cross my heart and hope to die.

She walks off. SANDRA *follows her.*

Scene Three

Open day at the Lagan Mill. Mid-April.

TOMMY (*his hands in plaster*) is sitting watching SANDRA *who is writing on a large sheet of paper with a felt-tip pen. A radio is playing, very loudly, 'Alternative Ulster' by the Belfast punk group Stiff Little Fingers.* KATE *is rushing about. She turns the radio down. Exits.* ARTHUR *comes in carrying prepared food. He grins at* TOMMY.

ARTHUR: Hiya, Tommy. Clap your hands. How're ye doin'?

TOMMY: Okay.

SANDRA: It's one way of stoppin' smokin', eh Tommy? Here ye are Arthur.

She pins up a sign. 'Get Your Non-Sectarian Nosh Here.' Sits down and begins writing again.

TOMMY: They'll make ye take that down. (SANDRA *shrugs.*) What time are the big nobs comin' in?

ARTHUR: They're comin' for lunch an' then they're havin' a look roun' the sections.

TOMMY: An' then they'll pat yiz all on the head an' tell ye what good children yiz all are.

ARTHUR: There's some real big nob comin' in. He's a Royal or somethin'.

TOMMY: He's not a Royal. He's from the Home Office. They're interested in this scheme. Yous should be boycottin' his visit, not feedin' his face.

ARTHUR: Sandra, you're supposed to be helpin' me.

SANDRA: In a minute. Houl yer horses.

ARTHUR: What are ye doin'?

SANDRA: Makin' an Irish welcome for the English civil servant.

KATE *comes in. Turns the radio off.*

KATE: Does anybody know where Maureen is? Sandra?

SANDRA: Haven't seen her.

KATE: It's not like her. She's never late.

SANDRA: What do ye think, Kate?

She holds up another sign. It says 'Never Mind What The Papers Say. We All Love Ye, Conn.'

KATE: Who's Conn?

SANDRA: The man from the Home Office.

KATE: His name is Jeremy Saunders. Who's Conn?

They all grin.

KATE: Okay. I'm a thick middle-class moron. Would somebody like to explain it to me?

MAUREEN *rushes in. She is carrying a Marks and Spencer carrier bag.*

MAUREEN: Sorry I'm late Kate.

KATE: That's all right. Are you all right?

MAUREEN: I had a message to do this mornin'. Forgot to tell ye.

KATE: Are you sure you're all right?

MAUREEN: Why shouldn't I be all right?

KATE: Do you know who Conn is?

MAUREEN: Conn who?

ARTHUR: It's a name for any English Civil Servant.

TOMMY: It's short for constipation, the shite you can't get rid of.

KATE: Are you planning to pin that up?

SANDRA: They'll never know what it means, an' they'll be too polite to ask.

KATE: It would be really embarrassing if this scheme didn't get a second year's funding because an English civil servant was brighter than you lot thought.

TOMMY: I'm away. See yiz all later.

KATE: Are you not staying to heckle?

TOMMY: We're stagin' a demonstration.

KATE: Outside.

TOMMY: We're protestin' about Mr Jeremy Saunders bein' here. Do you know his da owns the half of Cornwall or somewhere?

KATE: God give me strength.

TOMMY: You shoulda said no, Kate.

KATE: I didn't want this open day. I was told it had to take place. Will you tell the Party that I don't care if Jeremy Saunder's father owns all of Cornwall. All I care about is getting enough money to keep this place going for at least another year. While you lot are trying to change the face of the world, I am just trying to get the kids here through another rotten day.

TOMMY: Yer wrong, Kate.

KATE: I know I'm wrong. But it's the best I can think of till the revolution comes.

SANDRA: Yer both wrong. When we're all drawin' the pension there'll still be head-the-balls like him an' there'll still be well-meanin' people like you, an' nuthin' will be no different. Do ye know what this scheme is? It's a friggin' Government joyride. A good laugh for a year, an' then ye grow up.

KATE: Put your poster up, Sandra. If Mr Jeremy Saunders is intelligent enough to know what it means, he'll be too sophisticated to care.

She walks out. TOMMY *follows her.*

ARTHUR: Do ye know what they're talkin' about Maureen?

SANDRA: Maureen doesn't know what time of day it is. What's in the bag?

MAUREEN: None of your business. What's all the glasses for?

ARTHUR: Wine.

SANDRA: We get lectures about the demon drink, an' they can't manage a meal without a bottle of wine.

MAUREEN: Where's the wine?

ARTHUR: Kate has it hid away. She's no dozer.

SANDRA *looks in the Marks and Spencer's bag.*

MAUREEN: Put that down!

SANDRA: I was only lookin'.

MAUREEN: Well don't. Yer hands is all felt tip.

SANDRA: Well you show me then.

MAUREEN: Not now.

SANDRA: Arthur!

ARTHUR: What?

SANDRA: On yer bike!

ARTHUR: What?

SANDRA: Maureen wants to try on her new frock.

MAUREEN: I don't!

ARTHUR: I won't look.

SANDRA: Bugger off when yer told.

ARTHUR: I've a lot to do. Yiz have ten minutes.

SANDRA: Don't come back in till yer called.

ARTHUR *exits.*

SANDRA: Well, come on then. Let us see.

MAUREEN *takes an expensive matching outfit out of the bag. Jacket, skirt, trousers, top, shoes.*

SANDRA: You rob the meter or what?

MAUREEN: I've been savin' up since Christmas. I've always wanted this outfit. It was reduced in the sale. You can wear the skirt or the trousers with the jacket, swap them roun'.

SANDRA: Try it on.

MAUREEN: Kate might come in.

SANDRA: Kate hasn't got nuthin' we haven't got.

MAUREEN *takes off her skirt and shoes. Puts on the new jacket, skirt and shoes.*

MAUREEN: No mirror. Is it nice?

SANDRA: The jacket's awful big.

MAUREEN: It's the fashion. It's supposed to be big.

SANDRA: It would fit two. It'll come in handy later on . . . ach, fer God's sake, Maureen, I was only jokin'. Stop lookin' like a wet week all the time.

MAUREEN: I'm not sure about the colour. They had it in pink as well.

SANDRA: Ye can always get it changed.

MAUREEN: I want to wear it the day.

SANDRA: What for? Are ye hopin' Mr Saunders'll fall for ye an' offer ye a job in Stormont Castle?

KATE *comes in*

KATE: Oh, that's nice Maureen. Is it new?

MAUREEN: Why shouldn't it be new?

KATE: No reason . . . I . . .

MAUREEN: I've as much right to new clothes as the next one, so I have.

KATE: You look lovely.

MAUREEN: I look a sight. It's too big.

She takes the outfit off. Stuffs it back into the bag.

KATE: Careful. Don't crease it or they won't give you your money back.

KATE *takes the clothes out, folds them, puts them back into the carrier bag. ARTHUR comes in.*

ARTHUR: Hey Kate, the Law's back. They want to see you.

KATE: They've already checked the building twice. What do they want now?

ARTHUR: They never said. I suppose when Jeremy Saunders comes in the place'll be crawlin' with them.

KATE: Mr Saunders will have his own heavies in tow. Would you two give Arthur a hand with the food? I won't be long.

ARTHUR: What about the wine?

KATE: They won't be here for a while. We'll open it later.

ARTHUR: The red should be opened in advance.

KATE: There's plenty of time.

She exits.

SANDRA: Good try, Arthur.

ARTHUR: Do ye think they'll let us drink the leftovers?

SANDRA: Yer ever hopeful.

ARTHUR: Are ye not wearin' your new frock for them, Maureen?

MAUREEN: No.

SANDRA *puts her finger into one of the bowls, tastes the contents.*

SANDRA: Jeesus, Arthur, what's this?

ARTHUR: Cheese dip.

SANDRA: It's revoltin'.

ARTHUR: Try this one.

SANDRA: What is it?

ARTHUR: Celery, date an' walnut salad.

SANDRA: I hate dates.

ARTHUR: Do ye like cooked ham?

SANDRA: It's all right.

ARTHUR: Well do ye think ye could stop complainin' an' roll the ham up, put a cocktail stick through it an' sprinkle it with chopped parsley?

SANDRA: What for?

ARTHUR: Because it looks nicer that way, than lyin' flat on a plate.

SANDRA: They're gonna ate it, not take pictures of it.

ARTHUR: Maureen, will you do the ham? (*To* SANDRA.) You do the lettuce, it's all yer fit for.

SANDRA: Up yer nose Arthur.

KATE *comes in.*

SANDRA: Hey Kate, do the Law know there's a suspect device in Arthur's potato salad?

KATE: Would the two of you go outside for a moment. I want to talk to Maureen.

SANDRA: What's up?

KATE: Just do as you're told!

ARTHUR: Is there somethin' wrong, Kate?

KATE: Just go.

SANDRA: Do as yer told and ye'll live long enough, Arthur.

SANDRA *and* ARTHUR *leave.*

KATE: Is it true Maureen?

MAUREEN: Is what true?

KATE: I said I wanted to talk to you first. They gave me five minutes.

MAUREEN: How did they know it was me?

KATE: Oh Maureen, what got into you?

MAUREEN: How did they know?

KATE: When you ran out of the shop, there was a policeman across the street. He recognised you. He was in court the day Johnnie was put on probation. They went to your home, and Johnnie told them you were here.

MAUREEN: What's Johnnie doin' in the house? He should be at school.

KATE: Never mind that now. Why did you do it? What on earth possessed you?

MAUREEN: My fella's back in Belfast, he's been away for a month. I was goin' to see him the night. I wanted to look nice.

KATE: Why didn't you ask me? I could

have lent you something to wear.

MAUREEN: I wanted somethin' new. My own. I'm fed up wearin' other people's cast-offs . . . I didn't go in to do nuthin' . . . I only went in to look . . . I've been eyin' that suit fer months . . . I heard they was all reduced . . . I only went in to see . . . I was standin' there, tryin' to make up my mind . . . the jacket was still too dear, but I had enough saved for the skirt or the trousers . . . I thought maybe the skirt . . . he said I had nice legs . . . an' then this woman an' her daughter come up, an' the girl tried on one of the jackets . . . an' it was lovely on her so it was . . . an' she said . . . she said, 'Do ye think I should get the trousers or the skirt' an' the woman said, 'Get both, it's not every day you're seventeen . . .' I followed them roun' the shop . . . they bought matchin' shoes an' a top . . . the shoes were real leather, reduced til twelve pounds . . . everything she was wearin' was brand new. What did she need with more clothes? Her mother bought her the lot . . . wrote a cheque . . . I just walked behind them . . . watchin' . . . an' then they stopped at the blouses . . . they set the bag on the floor while they were lookin' . . . an' I just lifted it . . . an' I run . . . it's not even my size . . .

KATE: Oh Maureen, Maureen . . .

MAUREEN: They'll lock me up an' put Johnnie away, an it'll all be my fault . . .

KATE: I'll phone a solicitor, ask him to go to the station . . .

MAUREEN: I'm sorry . . . I don't know why I done it . . . it was wrong . . .

KATE: It's all wrong, and none of it is your fault, so stop apologising.

MAUREEN: I've let ye down, I'm sorry . . .

KATE: No, I've let you down . . . you know what my reaction was when the police told me? How could Maureen do this to me . . . my star pupil . . . I'm becoming more and more like them . . . expecting you to be grateful for nothing. Sandra's right. I might as well live on the moon for all I know. Everything I have taken for granted all my life, you have had to fight for. Ordinary things like a warm dry house, nice clothes, education, opportunity, choice. You have no choice. None of you have. Poverty on the dole, or poverty on a Youth Opportunities Programme. And if you're very good and aspire to be like us, we might even find you a job.

MAUREEN: I've no chance of gettin' a job in an office now, have I? Not with a police record.

KATE: Maureen, you are going to have to learn how to fight, or they'll destroy you . . . I'll phone for a solicitor.

KATE *goes to the phone. As she dials there are noises, shouts from the street outside.* TOMMY *rushes in.*

TOMMY: Maureen! It's your Johnnie! He's nicked the fuckin' police car. He's coked to the gills, ridin' it round and round the block. The army's in the next street. Somebody'd better stop him before they do . . .

MAUREEN: No!

She runs out. KATE *runs after her.* ARTHUR *come in. He is nervous, agitated.*

TOMMY: It's Johnnie.

ARTHUR: I know. I seen him.

They look out of the window.

TOMMY (*admiringly*): Jeesus, look at him. He's like the friggin' 'A' Team . . . go on ye wee bugger. You show them . . .

There is a rattle of gunfire, screams, shouts.

TOMMY: Jeesus Christ!

ARTHUR *turns away from the window, puts his hands on his head, walks abruptly to the kitchen. He lifts a lettuce, pulls it apart. He is shaking.*

TOMMY: What are ye doin'?

ARTHUR: Shreddin' lettuce . . . you shouldn't cut it ye know . . . it destroys the vitamin C content if ye use a knife.

He is very agitated. His head hurts as he tries to block the memory of being shot and the subsequent slow, painful recovery.

TOMMY: Arthur?

ARTHUR: There is no pain ye know . . . not when yer hurt that bad . . . the brain shuts down . . . it's what saves ye . . . the oul brain knows when you've had enough . . . when it's more than a body can take . . . an' it shuts down . . . that way ye don't die of shock . . . you know what the worst bit is? . . . when ye sort of come to . . . an' ye can hear, but ye can't see an' ye can't speak . . . I remember I was shit scared they might think I was dead an' bury me alive . . . I thought I'd go mad . . . I thought maybe I *was* dead . . . but I wasn't . . . I wasn't. You can be shot to bits an' not be dead . . .

TOMMY: Arthur . . . Arthur!

ARTHUR: What's happenin' out there?

TOMMY *looks out of the window again.*

TOMMY: The street's fulla kids, dozens of them. They're all over the place, screamin' shoutin' throwin' stones at the army and the police . . . the kids won't let them near the car . . . an' yer man Saunders has arrived, an' the Brits are tryin' to protect him, get his big Mercedes outa the street . . . it's like bedlam out there . . . I can't see . . .

SANDRA *comes in. She is carrying* MAUREEN. MAUREEN *is a horrific bloody mess.*

SANDRA (*quietly, without expression*): Lock the door.

TOMMY *locks the door.* SANDRA *sets* MAUREEN *on the chair below the hairdryer.* MAUREEN *sprawls grotesquely, half on the chair, half on the floor.*

SANDRA (*expressionlessly*): She run between the car an' the army.

ARTHUR: I know. We seen her.

There is a brief moment when he might offer SANDRA *comfort, when she might accept. Then* SANDRA *turns away, grabs hold of* MAUREEN *shakes her, screams.*

SANDRA: Ye stupid bitch, ye daft stupid bitch! Ye haven't the sense ye were born with!

ARTHUR: Sandra . . .

SANDRA: What are you lookin' at, face-ache!

ARTHUR: She's dead, Sandra.

SANDRA: I know she's friggin' dead. Her guts is everywhere. That's what dying's like. (*She shakes* MAUREEN.) This is what it's like. Do you hear me? It's not lovely, an' it's not romantic like in stupid friggin' plays!

ARTHUR: Don't, Sandra.

SANDRA: Nobody's ever gonna write poetry about you! Nobody!

ARTHUR: Don't. It's not right.

There is a loud hammering on the door.

SANDRA: Fuck off! If you let the Brits touch her, so help me, Arthur, I'll stove in yer steel plate . . .

KATE (*offstage*): Arthur, Sandra, Tommy, please . . . open the door . . .

SANDRA: Give them a signed statement. Tell them she done it for love.

KATE: Please let me in.

ARTHUR: Ye just can't keep her here, Sandra.

SANDRA: Why not? Nobody else wants her.

ARTHUR: Let Kate in, Tommy.

KATE: Please, open the door.

TOMMY: Are ye on yer own Kate?

Sounds of argument outside.

KATE: Yes.

TOMMY: Swear.

KATE: I swear. Please, let me in.

> TOMMY *opens the door.* KATE *comes in.* TOMMY *locks the door again.* KATE *looks at* MAUREEN. *Looks away.*

KATE: Move her out of that chair.

SANDRA: Put her back on the knittin' machine.

> ARTHUR *pushes the food and the glasses off the table on to the floor. Lifts* MAUREEN. *Lays her gently on the table.*

KATE: Cover her with something.

SANDRA: Look at her. Everybody should look at her.

TOMMY: Did they get Johnnie as well?

KATE: He got a few cuts from the windscreen, that's all.

TOMMY: Jammy wee bugger. He always did have the luck of the devil.

Hammering on the door.

SANDRA: Do you know what it'll say in the papers the morra? 'Shoplifter gets shot.'

Blackout

In the darkness SANDRA *sings quietly 'Wouldn't It Be Good To Be In Your Shoes Even If It Was For Just One Day'.* MAUREEN *is carried off stage by* ARTHUR. TOMMY *chants 'No Job Nothin' To Do, No Money, On The Bru'.* SANDRA *sings quietly 'We Are the Divis Girls We Wear Our Hair In Curls'.*

KATE *sings 'Damp, Damp, Damp,*

Damp, Damp, Damp, Damp, Damp'. ARTHUR *returns singing 'As I Was Out Walkin' Outside Divis Flats, Where the Happiest Tenants Are Surely the Rats'.*

In semi-darkness, KATE, ARTHUR, SANDRA *and* TOMMY *clear the stage, singing excerpts of the songs from the play, which merge into a distorted medley.*

Rats, rats, rats, rats, rats, rats, rats, rats.
What will it be when we leave school.
Will it be Ace schemes or Y.T.P.
No job after school. No future that's the rule.

Unemployment. Unemployment.

Hope it's work real work
We hope it's work real work
We hope it's work real work
And not the dole.

Old Mother Hubbard went to the cupboard
To get a piece of bread
She put her hand in the breadbin
And found something else instead
AUGH!

SANDRA *sings loudly, defiantly*

We are the Divis girls we wear our hair in curls
We wear our skinners to our knees
We do not smoke or drink
That's what our parent think
We are the Divis girls
We are the Divis Street crowd of rowdies
We are a nuisance to the public I agree
I agree!
See us stand and talk to each other
We are mates, we are great, we agree

KATE, ARTHUR *and* TOMMY *exit.* SANDRA *sits down on a chair, lights a cigarette.*

OR *alternatively:*

After Sandra's line ' . . . Shoplifter gets shot'

Blackout

MAUREEN *is carried off stage and there is no singing, only the sound of broken glass being swept up. (This is the sound that usually follows violence in Belfast.)*

Scene Four

Early May. The Belfast Arts Council Gallery. SANDRA *sitting smoking a cigarette.* ARTHUR *comes in. He is wearing the 'Compensation Day' suit casually (sleeves rolled back and an expensive T-shirt.) Already he looks more prosperous, more middle class.*

ARTHUR: What's the use of comin' til an art exhibition if ye don't look at the pictures.

SANDRA: I have looked at the pictures. They're a load of crap.

ARTHUR: The man what done them is downstairs. He's from Russia.

SANDRA: If he was from roun' here, nobody'd give them a second look. I've seen better at the primary school open day.

ARTHUR: Kate says people are payin' hundreds for them.

SANDRA: Why don't ye put in an offer fer one. You'll be gettin' yer money any day now, won't ye?

ARTHUR: I have it all earmarked.

SANDRA: You treatin' yerself till a brain transplant?

ARTHUR: I'm takin' over Larry's.

SANDRA: Yer what?

ARTHUR: I've made him an offer he can't refuse. I'm gonna do it all up. Serve good food.

SANDRA: Did they pack yer head with green cheese in the hospital? Ye'll go broke in a year.

ARTHUR: I'm gonna have candles on the tables an' a man playin' the accordion.

SANDRA: I'll take you home again, Kathleen.

ARTHUR: Real French stuff. Ye hafta get them in the mood.

SANDRA: They'll set fire til the tableclothes with the candles.

ARTHUR: Not if you were there.

SANDRA: Me?

ARTHUR: The family's gonna help me out, part time, till I get goin . . . but I need somebody full time . . . a supervisor . . . to keep an eye on the place while I'm doin' the cookin' . . . make sure my da keeps his hands outa the till.

SANDRA: What makes ye think I would keep my hands outa yer till?

ARTHUR: No point in robbin' a business if yer a partner . . .

SANDRA: A what?

ARTHUR: I mean proper . . . one of the family.

There is an awkward, embarrassed pause.

SANDRA: Arthur . . . will you just go away an' leave me alone. Yer wearin' me out.

ARTHUR: Suit yerself.

He walks away. SANDRA *sits for a moment.*

SANDRA: The one an' only time I ever wore a white lace frock Arthur, was for my first communion . . . an' my mother parades me down the road to get my photo tuk, an' she says to the photographer, 'Isn't our Sandra a picture? Won't she make a beautiful bride?' an' I told her I was never gonna get married, an' she got all dewy-eyed because she thought I wanted to be a nun . . . A bride of Christ, or forty years' hard labour . . . my mother thinks anything in between is a mortal sin . . . She married a big child like you, Arthur, an' what did it get her . . . eight kids an' twenty years' cookin' cleanin' an' survivin' on grants an' handouts . . . You're too like my da fer comfort. Fulla big plans that'll come to nuthin' because yer too soft an' yer too easy-goin' an' havin' all that money won't make ye any different. Whatever your da an' the rest of your ones don't steal from ye, the world will. They'll ate ye alive . . . You know what the big trick in this life is? It's knowin' what ye don't want, an' I don't want to be a back-seat joyrider, content to sit and giggle behind the fellas who do the stealin' an' the drivin' . . . I stole a car once . . . all by myself . . . I never told nobody, doin' it was enough . . . I just drove it roun' them posh steets in South Belfast until it ran outa petrol, an' then I walked home. Didn't need to boast about it the way the fellas do . . . just doin' it was enough . . . When the careers' officer come til our school, he asked me what I wanted to do, an' I says, 'I wanna drive roun' in a big car like yer woman outa Bonnie an' Clyde, an' rob banks,' an, he thought I was takin' a hand out him, so I says, 'All right then, I'll settle fer bein' a racin' driver.' An' he says, 'I'd advise you to settle for something less fantastic Sandra.' . . . They're all the same. They ask ye what ye wanta be, an' then they tell ye what yer allowed to be . . . Me wantin' to be a racin' driver is no more fantastical than Maureen believin' the fairy stories . . . dilly day-dream, just like her mother before her . . . somewhere over the rainbow, bluebirds die . . .

KATE *comes in.*

KATE: You know the best thing about this exhibition?

SANDRA: What?

KATE: The free wine.

SANDRA: Somebody's payin' for it. Nuthin's free.

KATE: Tommy's right. You should join the Party.

SANDRA: I went to visit Tommy on the way here.

KATE: How is he?

SANDRA: His left hand's okay. The right hand . . . they're gonna hafta break it an' reset some of the bones.

KATE: Oh God.

SANDRA: Lucky he's left handed . . . born klute as well as half-caste. God gave him a good start in life, didn't he . . . Did you get to read the report the hospital done on Maureen?

KATE: Yes.

SANDRA: What did it say?

KATE: It said that she died of gunshot wounds.

SANDRA: Did it say anything else about her?

KATE *pauses. They look at each other for a moment.*

KATE: Why didn't she tell me . . . Why didn't you tell me?

SANDRA: I thought maybe she imagined it. She was forever day-dreamin' . . . Have you ever been to the Botanic Gardens, Kate?

KATE: Yes. It's really lovely. As well as the park, there's a palm house and a tropical ravine, and the Ulster Museum . . . Would you like to go sometime?

SANDRA: No.

The lights dim to sound of Nik Kershaw recording of 'Wouldn't It Be Good To Be In Your Shoes.'